The International Ombudsman Yearbook
Volume 7, 2003

The International Ombudsman Yearbook Volume 7, 2003

Edited by

International Ombudsman Institute
Edmonton, Alberta, Canada

and

Linda C. Reif
Professor, Faculty of Law, University of Alberta,
Edmonton, Alberta, Canada

2005

MARTINUS NIJHOFF PUBLISHERS
LEIDEN / BOSTON

A C.I.P. Catalogue record for this book is available from the Library of Congress.

Printed on acid-free paper.

ISBN 90-04-14786-1
© 2005 *Koninklijke Brill NV, Leiden, The Netherlands*

Koninklijke Brill NV incorporates the imprints Brill Academic Publishers,
Martinus Nijhoff Publishers and VSP.

http://www.brill.nl

Printed and bound in The Netherlands.

THE INTERNATIONAL OMBUDSMAN INSTITUTE

The International Ombudsman Institute is a non-profit organization whose objects include promotion of the concept of ombudsmanship, encouragement and support of research in the ombudsman field, development of educational programs associated with ombudsmanship, the organization of international ombudsmanship conferences, and provision of a resource center for storage and dissemination of information about the ombudsman institution.

The International Ombudsman Yearbook, published annually by the International Ombudsman Institute and Martinus Nijhoff Publishers, is a multidisciplinary publication devoted to the study of the concept of ombudsmanship and the institution of the ombudsman, either in its classic or adapted form.

Contributions to the body of research and literature in the ombudsman field are welcomed from various disciplines including law, public administration, and political science.

Mr. Cheong U
Director
Commission Against Corruption
Macau
Alameda Dr. Carlos Assumpçáo
Edif. "Dynasty Plaza"
14 andar - NAPE
Macau, China

Australasia and Pacific

Mr. Bruce Barbour
Regional Vice-President
Ombudsman, New South Wales
Australia
Level 3, 580 George Street
Sydney, N.S.W. 2000, Australia

Mr. Ila Geno
Director
Chief Ombudsman, Papua New
Guinea
P.O. Box 852
Boroko, NCD, Papua New Guinea

Europe

Mr. Peter Kostelka
Regional Vice-President
Volksanwaltschaft
Singerstraße 17
AT 1015 Vienna, Austria

Ms. Riitta-Leena Paunio
Director
Parliamentary Ombudsman
Parliament Building Annex
Arkadiankatu 3
FI 00102 Helsinki, Finland

Mr. Matjaž Hanžek
Director
Human Rights Ombudsman
Dunajska 56
1109 Ljubjana, Slovenia

Latin America and Caribbean

Mr. Jose Luis Soberanes Fernandez
Regional Vice-President
Comisión Nacional de Derechos
Humanos, Mexico
Periferiso Sur. No. 3469, 5 piso
Col. San Jeronimo Lidice
C.P. 10200, Mexico D.F.

Dr. Eduardo Rene Mondino
Director
Defensor del Pueblo de la República
Argentina
Montevideo 1244
1018 Buenos Aires, Argentina

Dr. Hayden Thomas
Director
Ombudsman, Antigua/Barbuda
Deanery Place & Dickensonbay
Street, P.O. Box 204
St. John's, Antigua

North America

Mr. Howard Kushner
Regional Vice-President
756 Fort Street
P.O. Box 9039 Stn. Prov. Gov't.
Victoria, British Columbia, Canada
V8W 9A5

Mrs. Pauline Champoux-Lesage
Director
Le Protectrice du citoyen
525, boul. René-Lévesque Est.
Bureau 1.25, Québec City, Québec
Canada G1R 5Y4

GUIDELINES TO AUTHORS

1. We invite the submission of articles to be considered for publication. In general, articles should not exceed 100 double-spaced, typed pages in length, inclusive of endnotes.

2. Papers to be considered for publication must be sent to the Editor, *The International Ombudsman Yearbook*, International Ombudsman Institute, Faculty of Law, University of Alberta, Edmonton, Alberta T6G 2H5, Canada, <lreif@law.ualberta.ca>. Submission of a paper implies that it comprises original unpublished work. If possible, please submit the paper with a copy on computer diskette or by e-mail attachment. The International Ombudsman Institute uses Wordperfect 6, 7, 8, 9, 10 and 11.

3. Contributors are requested to keep an accurate copy of the manuscript in their possession since the *Yearbook* cannot assume responsibility for the safety of any manuscript sent to it or undertake to return it.

4. Manuscripts (text and endnotes) should be typewritten on one side of the paper only, double-spaced. Endnotes should be placed at the end of the text. All pages should be numbered consecutively. Titles and headings should be short. Extensive quotations in the text should be indented.

5. Cases, statutes, quotations, etc. must be cited accurately. Generally, please see the *Yearbook* for house style. The *Canadian Guide to Uniform Legal Citation* is used for law-related citations. Contributors are responsible for the accuracy of all citations and quotations and are requested to check them with particular care.

6. The Editor reserves the right to make alterations and corrections to conform both with the general style of the publication and accepted rules of grammar and syntax.

7. Galley proofs will be sent to authors and should be corrected clearly and returned to the address given by the date stated.

8. Authors will be provided with one free copy of the *Yearbook* containing their contribution. Authors should supply the address to which the copy of the *Yearbook* should be sent.

THE INTERNATIONAL OMBUDSMAN YEARBOOK
(2003) VOLUME 7

TABLE OF CONTENTS

FOREWORD

This publication is the seventh annual volume of *The International Ombudsman Yearbook*, compiled and edited by the International Ombudsman Institute and now produced by Martinus Nijhoff Publishers (formerly Kluwer Law International). During the 1980s and early 1990s, the publication was named *The International Ombudsman Journal* (1981-1994) numbers 1-12, renamed the *International Ombudsman Journal* (1995) for number 13, and was published annually.

The I.O.I. was established in 1978 with its secretariat at the Faculty of Law, University of Alberta, Edmonton, Alberta, Canada. The Board of Directors is comprised of ombudsmen representing all of the regions in the world. By the end of 2004, the Institutional Membership of the I.O.I. stood at 130 classical and human rights ombudsman offices, illustrative of the popularity of the institution both at national and sub-national levels of government. In 1996 the I.O.I. established a three-language publication policy, establishing English, French and Spanish as official I.O.I. languages. Where possible, I.O.I. publications are being translated into each of these languages. Although *The International Ombudsman Yearbook* is published mainly in English, each article in the *Yearbook* commences with an abstract of the article printed in the other two languages of the I.O.I.

The development of *The International Ombudsman Yearbook* was a result of the considerable increase in the number of ombudsman offices in the past thirty-five years, with a consequential increase in the interest in research and scholarship on the ombudsman concept. The classical model of the ombudsman office—a general jurisdiction public sector institution established by the legislative branch of government to monitor and regulate the administrative activities of the executive branch—was first established in its modern form in Sweden in 1809, and it then spread through Scandinavia in the first half of the twentieth century. Next, the office was established in Commonwealth and other countries starting in the 1960s and 1970s. The more recent transition to democratic governance in various countries around the world, associated in part with post-Cold War developments, has seen the institution established in many more countries in the past fifteen years, especially in Latin America, Central and East Europe, Africa and the Asia-Pacific area. The ombudsman model has been established at the international or supranational level of governance—the European Ombudsman was established in the Treaty on European Union (Maastricht Treaty). The ombudsman idea has also been adapted for use in various ways in particular government sectors and in the private sector, such in corporations, industries, colleges and universities.

The original word for the office—"ombudsman"—can be translated as meaning "representative". Many public and private sector offices around the world have maintained this title. However, a growing number of offices, particularly in the public sector, have adopted new terms to represent the office. These include *Defensor del Pueblo* (e.g. Spain, Argentina, Peru), Public Protector (South Africa), *Médiateur de la République* (e.g. France, Senegal) and Parliamentary Commissioner for Administration (e.g. United Kingdom, Sri Lanka).

The International Ombudsman Yearbook focuses primarily on the public sector ombudsman model. Articles included in the *Yearbook* examine various aspects of the institution from different disciplines, including law, political science and public administration. The scholarship is both theoretical and practical, as the audience interested in the ombudsman concept is composed of persons directly involved in the establishment and operation of ombudsman offices, scholars and others who are interested in the theoretical issues in the field.

Every four years, the I.O.I. holds an international ombudsman conference. The latest I.O.I. conference was held in Quebec City, Quebec, Canada on September 7-10, 2004. The theme of the Conference was "Balancing the Obligations of Citizenship with the Recognition of Individual Rights and Responsibilities—The Role of the Ombudsman". This volume of the *Yearbook* contains a selection of papers presented at the Conference, and includes the Opening Address delivered by Her Excellency the Right Honourable Adrienne Clarkson, Governor General of Canada, and a plenary address delivered by Mr. Justice Louis LeBel of the Supreme Court of Canada (in French). Other papers included in this Volume cover considerations on the establishment of a First Nations Ombudsman, demonstrating the value of an ombudsman, and the Charter of Rights of the European Union and its relevance for ombudsman institutions.

A list of "Contributors and Titles to *The International Ombudsman Yearbook* and to *The Ombudsman Journal* 1981-2003" can be found at the end of the volume. Copies of the earlier *Journals* can be purchased from the International Ombudsman Institute, Faculty of Law, Law Centre, University of Alberta, Edmonton, Alberta, T6G 2H5, Canada, e-mail: <dcallan@law.ualberta.ca>.

I would also like to thank Mrs. Diane Callan, International Ombudsman Institute Office Manager, and Ms. Megan Chorlton, LL.B. 2005, for their invaluable assistance in the work of editing and compiling this volume of *The International Ombudsman Yearbook*.

Professor Linda C. Reif
Editor, International Ombudsman Institute
Faculty of Law, University of Alberta

March 21, 2005

SPEECH ON THE OCCASIONAL OF THE OPENING OF THE VIIITH INTERNATIONAL CONFERENCE OF THE INTERNATIONAL OMBUDSMAN INSTITUTE

Her Excellency the Right Honourable Adrienne Clarkson*

I'm delighted, as Governor General of Canada, to welcome you to Quebec City, which is an architectural jewel, North America's only walled city, a UNESCO world heritage site, and a place full of *joie de vivre*. It is also a place of profound historical importance.

In 1759, a great battle fought near here was the decisive event in the British consolidation of their holdings in North America. English-speaking Protestants took over, by military force, a colony of francophone Roman Catholics, and the Treaty of Paris confirmed it. Just over ten years later, though, the *Quebec Act* was proclaimed. In it, the ruling British made an uncharacteristic exception for French Canada by not insisting that the population become English-speaking and Protestant.

At a time when British law barred Roman Catholics from holding office, the victors needed a way to make sure that the French population, who greatly outnumbered the British presence, could be brought into the councils of the colony. The *Quebec Act* formally re-established the Roman Catholic Church; instituted English criminal law alongside French civil codes regarding property; and provided for a government with an appointed legislative council for which Roman Catholics would be qualified.

Here, accommodation was the name of the game right from the start. Sometimes, we in Canada take for granted that this naturally happened and that statesmen were totally logical in their decision to behave this way. But as other examples in the world show us, such a compromise was one of the most remarkable

* Governor General of Canada.

things that happened in this country, and we are very proud of it even though we may not be sure why. It underlies our belief that we can remake our institutions, accommodate differences, and transform ourselves in a way that ethnically based nation states, particularly in Europe, can or will not. I remember when the idea of an ombudsman was first talked about in Canada a few decades ago. Most of us who were interested and involved in public policy understood this much, more or less: "the role of the Ombudsman is to protect the people against violation of rights, abuse of powers, error, negligence, unfair decisions and maladministration, to improve public administration and make the government's actions more open, and the government and its servants more accountable to members of the public."

In my personal view, the institution of the ombudsman should serve us all by making public administration and government actions more open. When the citizen comes in contact with the structures of her civic system, it is the citizen who must be served. The citizen comes first.

This is why you have such an important role to play, not just in reacting to complaint but also in promoting civic engagement. How can you and your staffs contribute to a greater societal awareness of your function? By putting the citizen first in your minds, you will contribute to the ongoing development of participatory democracy, because individuals and their communities are steadily learning how to involve themselves in making their corners of the world operate decently, fairly, and democratically. Especially among young people, we need to overcome apathy and a sense of remoteness from democratic institutions, which depend on widespread participation.

The International Ombudsman Institute is a good example of the institutions that are rising to meet the needs of a world that feels ever smaller, even though its administration seems more complicated and, often, intimidating. The word "ombudsman" comes from an Old Norse word meaning "representative", suggesting that this office represents and acts for the individual citizen. We follow, then, in the footsteps of the Swedes, who installed in 1809 a supervisory agency which was independent of the executive branch and designed to restrain autocratic tendencies.

Our State visits to northern Europe last year showed all our delegation the kind of society that can be created with the ombudsman as a very active part. Iceland has a separate ombudsman for adults, for youth and children, and for the disabled. Finland has six—a parliamentary ombudsman, and one each concerned with equality, data protection, minorities, consumers, and bankruptcy. Sweden, the pioneer, has seven ombudsmen serving a catalogue of groups and interests that all progressive societies are trying to learn how to protect: freedom and responsibility of the press, consumers, children and youth, the disabled, ethnic minorities, minority sexual orientations, as well as equal opportunities for citizens generally.

By unfortunate contrast, very few countries in Africa and Asia even have such a position; the United States has fewer than ten public-sector ombudsmen, most of them at the municipal level. We're proud that Clare Lewis, your Institute's

5

president, is one of ten Canadian ombudsmen—each one attached to one of our provincial legislatures. Our provinces of Alberta and New Brunswick were the first to institute the position in 1967 and Clare Lewis's province of Ontario followed suit in 1975. We can also be proud that the International Ombudsman Institute is housed at the University of Alberta in Edmonton.

The work of ombudsmen to protect the rights of the citizen *vis-à-vis* the structures of government is important, but it remains relatively recent. It forms part of the worldwide movement to recognize and safeguard the rights and rightful place of the individual citizen. The great English philosopher, John Stuart Mill, said this in his still-relevant and startling essay "On Liberty" 145 years ago: "No society in which these liberties are not, on the whole, respected, is free, whatever may be its form of government; and none is completely free in which they do not exist absolute and unqualified. The only freedom which deserves the name is that of pursuing our own good in our own way, so long as we do not attempt to deprive others of theirs, or impede their efforts to obtain it. Each is the proper guardian of his own health, whether bodily, or mental and spiritual. Mankind are greater gainers by suffering each other to live as seems good to themselves, than by compelling each to live as seems good to the rest."

Here in Canada in 2003, the Right Honourable Beverly McLachlin, Chief Justice of Canada, put it this way in the Baldwin-LaFontaine lecture: "Rights, like the nation state, create a protected space for difference within society; a space within which communities of cultural belonging can form and flourish under the broad canopy of civil society."

This protection for difference within society is very evident here in Canada. Through our history—I have already told you about the *Quebec Act* 230 years ago—we have made diversity work. More immediately, our immigration and refugee policies of the past forty years have brought breathtaking changes to Canadian life.

When I arrived here with my family as a refugee in 1942, I came to a white country with white people, white bread, and white institutions. Now, our country is an astonishing mix of cultural richness. Consider something as simple and profound as food, for example. We take for granted in Canada that we can have a falafel for lunch and sushi for dinner. In fact, one of the common observations of young people travelling to Europe for the first time is that the food in each country is good, but rather uniform; they have grown up with a variety of ways to encounter different cultures through the simple act of eating. This is just one small aspect of our growth in celebrating and harnessing our capacity for difference. It has helped us to understand that there are wonderful things other than what we have, and marvellous people who are not quite like what we are. The balance we seek is to do this without sacrificing essential principles and foundational values.

We have not had an unbroken path towards this acceptance of diversity. We had racially-based immigration laws until the late fifties. We took away the civil rights and property of people of Japanese origin during the Second World War, even when they had been born here. Canada still grapples with the important relationship with its Aboriginal peoples after centuries-long attempts to assimilate or isolate them, especially regarding frequently-violated treaties which surrendered land to the settlers.

I am certain that the greatest service Canada can offer to the world, as we continue to bring this extraordinary and exemplary society into being, is to not just tolerate difference but to welcome it and to show how it enriches our lives.

I want to tell you a little bit about the role of the Governor General in the Canadian system. Its evolution has placed the Canadian Head of State in an interesting position. Constitutionally, the Governor General has certain responsibilities, most often symbolic in character; the Office is called upon to exercise power only in ensuring that the country always has a Prime Minister to lead the government. Such a critical intervention has happened only twice in our history. More typically, the Governor General presides over the government in a ceremonial way, leaving the business of government to elected officials. That is how the role of the Governor General has been constitutionally conceived.

As the role has been culturally lived, though, as Governor General I have several duties: to encourage Canadians to excellence; to promote, in a clearly non-partisan way, their engagement in the civic life of their communities and their country; and to nourish the very best kinds of public conversation. In the last year, I have attended 917 events in more than eighty communities. In addition, I represent Canada abroad on State visits, and last year I went to Russia, Finland and Iceland; the year before to Germany and the year before that to Chile and Argentina. I do this at the request of the Prime Minister and the Ministry of Foreign Affairs in order to enhance Canada's relationship with other nations.

These functions have evolved over the decades and continue to change. What may be constant to the Governor General's experience, however, is how valuable it is to people who feel that they have been heard through its agency. I'm sure that you also experience, in your work, how important it is for people to be acknowledged and understood. One small example of this can be found in the tide of unsolicited letters and electronic mail that we receive at Rideau Hall. There are messages of general support and encouragement, and to be sure, there is criticism. But there is also a regular, sometimes heartbreaking flow of submissions from troubled people who don't know where to turn. Their difficulties are with the legal system, with refugee or immigration requests, with government agencies or with an estranged spouse—all the trials and misfortunes of living life in the modern world lead them to call out for assistance from the Governor General.

Most often these are matters in which the Governor General cannot become involved, and my staff works hard to point the writers in helpful directions—the appropriate agency or ministry, including, of course, the provincial ombudsmen. Our experience has been that the need for citizen advocacy and for a better understanding of the role of the ombudsman is very clear.

I've also been privileged to hear Canadians in every walk of life, from the homeless to the philanthropic well-to-do. A major emphasis of my mandate has been to create forums in which their points of view can be shared and respected. Canada's young leaders, Inuit and Aboriginal communities, high school graduating classes, community activists—all have been engaged in roundtable conversations, most recently on what makes and will make our cities good places to live. One of the chief roles of my Office, then, as I see it, is to foster dialogue. As long as people keep talking—and keep *listening*—and keep having what I call "safe conversations" with each other, they enrich their commitment to their communities as well as their sense of national belonging. This may be essential to your function, as well.

It is vital in a country like ours. Our national objective is to accept immigrants at the rate of one percent of our population each year. We don't quite get to that level, but we do take in well over 200,000 immigrants annually, and it has transformed our country. Newcomers can join this national conversation right away, because our immigrants are chosen with the intention that they will become Canadian citizens within three to five years. They are not squatters; they just have a little less seniority than the rest of us! They will learn French or English and a certain amount of Canadian history and then away they go. Citizenship is the most fundamental institution—a promise of rights and a call to duty—for human beings living within a state. All people must have the chance to become citizens where their work and their lives are made. This is the underlying civic belief in Canada, one that we have come to through experiment and social transformation.

Your theme—"Balancing the Obligations of Citizenship with the Recognition of Individual Rights and Responsibilities"—goes straight to the heart of what has always been sought in civic life. What is the duty owed by a citizen to the state? What are the rights of the citizen in a civil and democratic society? In a time when institutionalized selfishness and marketplace greed are rampant, the insistent and constant honouring of our basic humanity is important. While too much state or corporate power is an obvious problem, unrestrained individualism also carries a curse: a chronic sense of grievance, of perpetual entitlement, of civic ignorance, and a wilful disregard for history.

As ombudsmen, you have been assigned to moderate governmental authority through advocacy on behalf of individuals and groups. You are at the centre of our society's attempts to balance these duties and rights.

An urgent and timely debate is treated in your third plenary session, in which you will weigh the maintenance of human rights with needs for national and international security and watchfulness. Everyone is worried about this and the balance is delicate. This doesn't mean that there won't be grey areas and misapplications of principle—our own country has often experienced them in the last century—but a healthy and open society will right itself and minimize the damage of even the most woeful situation.

One of the most exciting aspects of a conference like this is that you are a learning organization, one that can grow because of the accumulated knowledge of its members and which can be of practical benefit to citizens around the world.

I hope it will allow your Institute to truly know and use what is being learned by your diverse constituent parts, thereby giving each of you a clearer vision and an improved ability to do your job. From my perspective as an outsider, it seems to me that there are two venues in which to use this learning.

One is internal. There is a continual need for professional development in the face of the complex human problems that your staffs encounter. Recently, a noted Canadian advocate for refugees, Mary Jo Leddy, said this: "Our system should be oriented toward one thing only, that is, the formation of good citizens." Among the problems she sees, apart from limited resources within the apparatus of citizenship and immigration, is that there are two distinct levels of comprehension within the system. Some staff come in with extensive education and overseas experience and therefore understand the sources from which refugee situations arise. Others, though, who rise in the system with little background outside the bureaucracy, can be reflexively suspicious, with the result that potentially valuable citizens have their lives placed on hold for years. When those delays happen, we have what Leddy refers to as "a loss of social capital".

Now, I don't know what your staffs are like and how you put them together, but there is always the challenge of helping people—especially anyone who deals directly with the public—to develop skills in human relations, as well as a very clear and broad view of what your office is trying to achieve. You need people with sophistication of the spirit and a heartfelt vision. Facts and protocols and technical skills can easily be taught, but these other qualities must be sought and nurtured, for they will make all the difference to your work and the development of your offices.

I've often said that there are only two kinds of societies—those that punish and those that forgive. I like to think that we have a forgiving society in Canada. For all our errors we have, since even before our formal Confederation in 1867, preferred discourse, accommodation, and transformation over the nourishment of grudges and the politics of punishment. This movement towards the development of forgiving societies is one in which your Institute can make a real and growing contribution.

As you do your work here in Quebec City, I return to the words of J.S. Mill: "Civil, or Social Liberty—the nature and limits of the power which can be legitimately exercised by society over the individual—[is] a question seldom stated, and hardly ever discussed, in general terms, but which profoundly influences the practical controversies of the age ... and is likely soon to make itself recognized as the vital question of the future."

In a conference such as this, you are examining and striving to meet one of the most vital needs of civilization. I wish you all speed and strength and hope in your deliberations, and as you return to your work. Again, welcome to Canada and to Quebec City, and to thoughts of the better society that we are all trying to build.

DÉMOCRATIE ET PROTECTION DE LA DIVERSITÉ CULTURELLE

Monsieur le juge Louis LeBel*

The author discusses the problem of the relationship between democratic values and the reception of cultural diversity in contemporary democracies. First, it is asserted that our modern understanding of democratic ideals should make room for the accommodation of cultural diversity. International law appears to be moving in that direction, although it remains unsettled and its evolution is far from over. The Canadian experience, since the birth of the Canadian Confederation, underlines the possibility of this kind of accommodation. Nevertheless, democratic states must retain a commitment to a set of shared fundamental values which ought to be accepted by all cultural communities. Ombudsmen and public mediator are called upon to play a critical part in this difficult process of accommodation between contemporary democratic societies and the different grants which have found a place within them.

****

El autor discute el problema de las relaciones entre los valores democráticos y la diversidad cultural en las democracias contemporáneas. En primer lugar, se asevera que nuestra comprensión moderna de los ideales democráticos debiera dejar lugar para la adaptación a la diversidad cultural. La ley internacional parece tender a dirigirse en esa dirección, aunque no ha sido establecida y su evolución está lejos de estar terminada. La experiencia canadiense, desde el nacimiento de la Confederación Canadiense, destaca la posibilidad de este tipo de adaptación. Sin embargo, los estados democráticos deben mantener un compromiso con un

* C'est allocution etait présenter a L'huitième congrès de l'institut international de l'ombudsman, Centre des Congrès, Québec, Septembre 7 au 10, 2004.

conjunto de valores fundamentales compartidos que deberían ser aceptados por todas las comunidades culturales. Se convoca a los ombudsmen y al mediador público a desempeñar un rol crítico en este proceso difícil de adaptación entre las sociedades democráticas contemporáneas y las distintas concesiones que han sido aceptadas en ellas.

Introduction

L'évolution du sens de la démocratie

Tel que je l'avais indiqué, j'entends aujourd'hui faire quelques observations sur ce thème très général et très discuté "Démocratie et protection de la diversité culturelle". L'idée que je me fais de la démocratie est qu'il est possible et désirable de protéger la diversité culturelle dans une démocratie moderne. En effet, je tends à accepter une vision communautaire de la démocratie selon laquelle on peut respecter les droits fondamentaux du citoyen tout en reconnaissant, parfois au moyen d'obligations juridiques positives, les demandes de reconnaissance politique ou sociale des minorités culturelles présentes au sein de l'État-nation.

La diffusion de cette idée de la démocratie, qui accepte dans une large mesure la légitimité démocratique de la diversité culturelle, reste néanmoins un phénomène récent dans le monde moderne. Autrefois, la démocratie était considérée comme un mécanisme de *fusion* de la diversité, grâce aux valeurs de liberté et d'égalité juridique. Notre compréhension de ce concept de démocratie comporte maintenant une véritable reconnaissance et une acceptation authentique de la différence, sous toutes ses formes, linguistique, religieuse, politique, raciale, ou autre.

Évidemment, l'idée que la démocratie est censée reconnaître la diversité culturelle ne fait toujours pas l'unanimité dans l'ensemble des États démocratiques.

L'auteur désire remercier Me Nigel Marshman, avocat à Ottawa, auxiliaire juridique à la Cour suprême du Canada au cours de l'année judiciaire 2003-2004, pour sa collaboration dans la préparation et la rédaction des notes.

En fait, dans notre monde démocratique, coexistent, en gros, deux visions de la démocratie et de la citoyenneté. La première vision de la démocratie est celle que partagent la majorité des Américains et des Français. Dans ces pays, la démocratie est considérée comme un instrument d'assimilation et on y encourage publiquement les citoyens à accepter un ensemble unique de valeurs culturelles et politiques. Aux États-Unis on parle du "melting pot", alors qu'en France, on invoque le "modèle républicain"[1] d'intégration. Dans cette vision, le citoyen est considéré comme une personne qui, avec le temps, adopte les valeurs politiques et culturelles partagées par la nation dans son ensemble. Bien qu'il puisse jouir certaines libertés individuelles dans sa vie privée quant à sa culture, le citoyen n'est aucunement reconnu publiquement ou politiquement comme appartenant à une culture distincte,

11

différente de celle de l'État dans son ensemble.

Le Canada souscrit en grande partie aujourd'hui à une vision communautaire de la démocratie. C'est le cas dans d'autres pays comme la Belgique, la Suisse, l'Afrique du Sud, et l'Inde. Cette forme de démocratie reconnaît dans une plus grande mesure la diversité, notamment la diversité culturelle, comme susceptible de relever de la sphère de la vie publique et non pas seulement du domaine de la vie privée.

Selon la vision communautaire de la démocratie, la diversité est acceptée dans la plus grande mesure possible, sans toutefois porter atteinte au sens de citoyenneté commune nécessaire à la préservation de la société civile dans son ensemble et à la vie des états qui encadrent celle-ci. Cette conciliation ne se réalise pas toujours sans mal. L'expérience démontre qu'elle exige de nombreux compromis, l'empathie, et l'ouverture d'esprit.

Si un observateur étranger, en particulier celui qui appartient à la tradition républicaine, examine l'exemple du Canada et son expérience historique, il sera peut-être déconcerté de constater dans quelle mesure nous admettons ou commençons à reconnaître la diversité culturelle présente dans notre État fédéral. Cet observateur sera tenté de ne voir dans le Canada qu'un enchevêtrement incompréhensible d'allégeances. Les deux peuples fondateurs, les Français et les Anglais, tentent de vivre ensemble. Les Autochtones demandent la pleine reconnaissance de leurs droits, notamment une forme d'autonomie gouvernementale. De plus, l'État canadien a intentionnellement juxtaposé à cette interaction entre les intérêts culturels des Français, des Anglais et des Autochtones, une politique de multiculturalisme conçue afin de permettre à la population immigrante extrêmement diversifiée du Canada de prospérer et de ne pas disparaître. S'ajoutent à cette combinaison des différences culturelles régionales importantes, dans l'Ouest ou dans les Maritimes, que le système fédéral canadien ne reconnaît qu'en partie.

On ne s'étonnera pas alors que deux des philosophes contemporains les plus connus par leurs réflexions sur le communautarisme et la reconnaissance des différents types de citoyenneté soient des Canadiens, Charles Taylor et Will Kymlicka. Ces deux intellectuels réputés ont fait beaucoup pour démontrer que, malgré la nature parfois complexe d'une démocratie communautaire et les tensions qu'elle engendre parfois, il est possible de reconnaître les différences culturelles et d'aménager leur coexistence à l'intérieur d'un État qui demeure malgré tout viable.

Charles Taylor, par exemple, admet volontiers les difficultés inhérentes au modèle communautaire de démocratie. Que la protection d'une collectivité au sein de l'État canadien devienne une priorité publique implique toujours un risque de méconnaissance des droits individuels des personnes qui ne partagent pas toutes les idées ou valeurs de leur communauté. Cette tâche n'est cependant pas insurmontable. Une démocratie communautaire demeure une démocratie libérale où les droits culturels et les droits collectifs doivent coexister avec les droits fondamentaux comme le droit à la vie, à la liberté, à l'égalité, à l'application régulière de la loi, à la liberté d'expression, ou à la liberté de religion. Lorsque certains droits fondamentaux entrent en conflit avec ceux de la communauté culturelle, l'État doit essayer de trouver un équilibre délicat, mais qui peut exiger l'atténuation, le cas échéant, de certaines exigences communautaristes. Une société civile doit demeurer capable de réaliser ces équilibres en prenant en compte les droits culturels collectifs d'une part et des droits individuels d'autre part. En tant qu'ombudsman ou médiateurs publics, dans des sociétés de plus en plus diverses, vous devez tous, j'en suis convaincu, concilier quotidiennement divers intérêts tout aussi importants les uns que les autres pour assurer le règlement équitable de cas souvent délicats ou pénibles. Il en va de même pour la démocratie communautaire. Dans son cadre, il faut alors apprendre, en tant que citoyens et en tant que société politique, à composer avec le type de "diversité profonde" qui existe au Canada ainsi que dans de nombreux états démocratiques modernes.

Les critiques de la vision communautaire de la démocratie craignent que les mesures destinées à favoriser la diversité culturelle au niveau politique affaiblissent ou même détruisent les liens inhérents à une citoyenneté commune en matière de citoyenneté. Selon ces critiques, la reconnaissance de la différence culturelle et celle de droits collectifs en faveur de minorités culturelles ne corrigent des injustices ou des inégalités apparentes qu'aux dépens d'un sentiment d'appartenance collectif national, puisqu'elle réaffirme et renforce la volonté de conserver et d'intensifier l'attachement à la communauté.

Peut-être parce que je suis Canadien et juge canadien, je suis devenu plutôt sceptique à l'égard de la validité d'une véritable vision intégrationniste en matière de citoyenneté, au moins dans le contexte de la vie de mon pays, mais sans doute aussi dans celui d'un monde de plus en plus divers et traversé de conflits culturels, malgré la globalisation qui prétend l'unir et l'uniformiser. Les modèles de démocratie communautaire semblent présenter des avantages importants dans un monde qui n'est peut-être pas aussi intégré qu'on le croit. Par contre, je suis prêt à reconnaître que la vision communautaire se heurte au problème de l'identification et de la consolidation d'une assise de valeurs communes.

Dans un grand nombre de démocraties aussi ou plus diversifiées que le Canada, le simple choix entre l'assimilation forcée ou l'intégration par l'effet d'une indifférence bénigne n'est tout simplement pas une option viable. Ces formes d'intégration sont souvent perçues par les communautés culturelles qu'elles visent comme un avenir intolérable pour ces minorités, puisque l'on cherche à nier des caractéristiques qui ont structuré profondément leur existence collective comme la vie individuelle de leurs membres. Il n'est certes pas facile de reconnaître le type de "diversité profonde"dont parle Charles Taylor mais cela doit et peut être tenté, en dépit des difficultés et des tensions propres à ces efforts communs d'une société civile. À ce propos, il importe toutefois de se souvenir que l'expérience historique démontre parfois que la capacité d'une démocratie communautaire de reconnaître la diversité culturelle au niveau politique peut créer et consolider une identité nationale commune forgée autour de la volonté de préserver une raison publique commune dans la vie sociale en consolidant des valeurs de respect mutuel, d'empathie et de tolérance.

La protection à l'échelle internationale des diversités culturelles en tant qu'expression de la démocratie

J'ai parlé jusqu'à maintenant de la nécessité de protéger la diversité culturelle au sein de l'État-nation démocratique. Au-delà des cadres de celui-ci, j'ai toutefois le sentiment que la communauté *internationale* évolue prudemment dans le sens de la protection de la diversité culturelle, en dépit de la persistance de modèles distincts de société démocratique.

Aux Nations-Unies, durant les premières années de son existence, l'accent, dans le domaine des droits de la personne, a indubitablement été plus axé sur l'interdiction de la discrimination contre les personnes, sur une base individuelle. La *Déclaration universelle des droits de l'homme* de 1948, par exemple, ne garantit pas expressément, au sens collectif, les droits des minorités ethniques, religieuses ou linguistiques. Cependant, comme je le mentionne un peu plus loin, dans le contexte canadien, l'interdiction de discrimination contre les personnes représente toujours une question de la plus grande importance. Il s'agit d'une composante essentielle des valeurs démocratiques nécessaires à la reconnaissance de la diversité culturelle, puisque souvent les phénomènes de discrimination se rattachent à des facteurs tels que la race, la religion, la langue, ou l'origine nationale. Ainsi, bien qu'ils aient été axés vers la protection des individus, il ne faut pas sous-estimer l'importance d'instruments internationaux comme la *Déclaration universelle des droits de l'homme* des Nations-Unies, dans la reconnaissance graduelle des diversités culturelles.

Avec le temps cependant, le sort des minorités et non plus seulement celui des individus appartenant à celles-ci a reçu une plus grande attention sur la scène internationale. C'est ainsi qu'a été adopté l'article 27 du *Pacte international relatif aux droits civils et politiques*, qui interdit de priver les minorités ethniques, religieuses et linguistiques du droit de jouir de leur propre culture, de professer et de pratiquer leur propre religion ainsi que de se servir de leur propre langue. L'article 27 revêt un intérêt particulier parce qu'il demeure un des rares outils juridiques internationaux destiné précisément à légitimer la reconnaissance de la différence culturelle.

L'efficacité de l'article 27 du *Pacte international relatif aux droits civils et politiques* reste cependant incertaine. Il semble que les rédacteurs de l'article ne voulaient pas imposer des obligations positives aux États, comme celle d'établir des écoles spéciales pour les personnes appartenant à des minorités linguistiques. Cet article a toutefois été invoqué avec succès par une femme autochtone canadienne dans la décision *Lovelace c. Canada*[2]. Cette femme avait perdu son droit de vivre sur une réserve indienne après avoir épousé un citoyen non-indien. Le Comité des droits de l'homme des N.-U. a tranché en sa faveur en concluant qu'il avait été porté atteinte à son [TRADUCTION] "droit [...] d'avoir accès à sa culture et à sa langue autochtone "en commun avec les autres membres" de son groupe" parce qu'il ne se trouvait au Canada aucun autre endroit en dehors de sa réserve où une telle collectivité existait. Par conséquent, l'article 27 du *Pacte international relatif aux droits civils et politiques* a été utilisé, d'une manière indirecte, afin de protéger la culture et la langue autochtone, en exigeant que cette femme autochtone ait accès à sa collectivité traditionnelle.

Plus récemment, on a tenté de renforcer l'article vingt sept du *Pacte international relatif aux droits civils et politiques*, grâce au paragraphe 2(1) de la *Déclaration sur les droits des personnes appartenant à des minorités nationales ou ethniques, religieuses et linguistiques*, qui a été adoptée en 1992 (en passant, cette Déclaration a été le premier instrument international entièrement consacré aux droits des minorités). En effet, le paragraphe 2(1) de cette Déclaration entend accorder aux minorités nationales ou ethniques, religieuses et linguistiques, le droit de jouir de leur culture, de professer et de pratiquer leur religion et d'utiliser leur langue, *en privé et en public*, en toute liberté et sans aucune ingérence ou forme de discrimination.

L'article premier de cette même *Déclaration* dispose que les États "protègent l'existence et l'identité nationale ou ethnique, culturelle, religieuse ou linguistique des minorités, sur leurs territoires respectifs, et favorisent l'instauration des conditions propres à promouvoir cette identité." Le paragraphe 1(2) poursuit en prévoyant expressément que les États adoptent les mesures législatives ou autres qui sont nécessaires pour parvenir à ces fins.

La lecture des dispositions de cette *Déclaration* nous ramène à la vision communautaire de la démocratie que j'ai évoquée plus haut. Dans *cet* instrument international en particulier qu'est la *Déclaration sur les droits des personnes appartenant à des minorités nationales ou ethniques*, on tente à tout le moins de garantir un degré de reconnaissance publique, c'est-à-dire de reconnaissance politique d'un droit à la diversité culturelle, plutôt que de limiter l'application de ce "droit" au domaine purement privé, comme le souhaitent souvent les tenants du modèle républicain ou intégrationniste.

Alors que la collectivité internationale dans son ensemble progresse ainsi vers la reconnaissance politique de la diversité culturelle, l'Union européenne semble également s'orienter dans cette direction. Plusieurs pays de l'Union européenne ont, évidemment, vécu sous la protection juridique de la *Convention européenne de sauvegarde des droits de l'homme et des libertés fondamentales* depuis les années cinquante. Bien qu'elle porte d'abord sur la reconnaissance et la défense des droits individuels, cette convention sauvegarde déjà en partie la diversité culturelle en Europe, dans le domaine privé, grâce à la protection qu'elle accorde à la liberté personnelle, à la vie privée et à la vie familiale, à la liberté de pensée, de conscience et de religion, à la liberté d'expression, à la protection contre la discrimination, et au droit à l'instruction. Il s'agit là indiscutablement de droits importants puisque la liberté individuelle de se livrer à des pratiques culturelles dans le domaine privé représente un élément essentiel à la croissance et à l'émancipation des collectivités.

La protection prévue dans la *Convention* quant au droit à l'instruction présente un caractère intéressant car elle tente, dans une certaine mesure, d'imposer des obligations positives à l'État à cet égard. L'article 2 du Protocole n° 1 prévoit, en effet, que nul ne peut se voir refuser le droit à l'instruction. Il exige également que l'État respecte le droit des parents d'assurer cette éducation et cet enseignement conformément à leurs convictions religieuses et philosophiques. Par exemple, dans l'affaire *Valsamis c. Greece*[3], la Cour européenne des droits de l'homme a conclu que l'article 2 implique l'existence de certaines obligations positives de la part des États dans ce domaine. Bien que l'étendue de ces obligations positives n'ait pas encore été établie par la Cour européenne[4], la reconnaissance de leur existence témoigne d'une acceptation croissante de la diversité culturelle et de la nécessité de sa protection en droit international.

Plus récemment, l'Union européenne a tenté, par la *Charte européenne des langues régionales ou minoritaires* (entrée en vigueur le 1er mars 1998), de protéger les personnes qui parlent des langues minoritaires. Cette convention demande la protection des "langues régionales et minoritaires", et, dans une moindre mesure, la protection des "langues non-territoriales"[5]. Cette Charte est le premier instrument international qui vise expressément à la protection des langues minoritaires. Sa portée dépend dans une grande mesure de la volonté de coopération des états membres, mais elle leur impose quelques obligations positives de veiller à la survie des collectivités linguistiques minoritaires à l'intérieur de leurs frontières[6]. Fait intéressant, la France, en dépit de son attachement à son modèle républicain de société, avait décidé de ratifier la *Charte européenne des langues régionales ou minoritaires*. Toutefois, le Conseil constitutionnel a décidé qu'une telle ratification n'était pas possible sans modification préalable de la Constitution de la République française. Ce type de conciliation linguistique fait toujours l'objet d'une controverse en France[7].

On voit que la *tolérance* de la différence, qu'elle soit culturelle, linguistique, religieuse ou autre, est de plus en plus courante en droit international, notamment lorsque cette conciliation se limite au domaine privé. On constate cependant que peu d'instruments internationaux exigent que les États reconnaissent publiquement et positivement les minorités culturelles, linguistiques et religieuses à l'intérieur de leurs frontières. Sur la scène internationale, ce type de reconnaissance demeure le plus souvent, dans l'ensemble, la seule prérogative de l'État-nation.

Ces réflexions m'amènent maintenant à traiter à nouveau de la situation canadienne. Comme je l'ai mentionné, le Canada s'est orienté de plus en plus nettement vers une vision communautaire de la démocratie. Notre pays adopte peu à peu un modèle de démocratie qui se refuse à définir étroitement et uniformément ce qu'est un Canadien.

Une expérience en matière de reconnaissance de la diversité culturelle: le cas du Canada

Je n'ai aucune réticence à évoquer ici l'expérience canadienne. Le Canada a certainement ses problèmes. Il a vécu des périodes de conflits, parfois intenses. Néanmoins, il possède une longue tradition de reconnaissance de la diversité culturelle, même dans le domaine public.

Le Canada, dès son origine, a admis la nécessité de respecter et de tolérer la diversité culturelle au sein de l'État-nation, et ce, malgré qu'il ait vu le jour dans une ère de nationalisme ethnique, d'intolérance linguistique et religieuse ainsi que de racisme. Lorsqu'à la fin de la guerre de sept ans, en 1763, le traité de Paris a cédé le Canada à la Grande-Bretagne, la population française de la vallée du Saint-Laurent était déjà trop importante et trop profondément enracinée pour qu'on ignore ses traditions et ses caractères culturels, ou encore, pour qu'on la déporte, comme les Britanniques l'avaient déjà fait dans l'Est avec la population acadienne, à partir de 1755, au cours de ce que l'on appellerait aujourd'hui une opération de nettoyage ethnique. Après une courte période à partir de 1763, au cours de laquelle le gouvernement britannique tenta de mettre en place une politique d'assimilation, en 1774, le parlement de Londres adopta l'*Acte de Québec* qui a alors permis à la population de langue française du Québec de conserver sa langue, sa religion et sa tradition de droit civil. L'adoption de l'*Acte de Québec* s'explique sans doute par des motifs forts pragmatiques. Ceux-ci tenaient beaucoup plus aux inquiétudes causées aux autorités impériales par les prodromes de la révolution américaine et à la nécessité de s'assurer de la fidélité et du calme de la population francophone du Canada et de son clergé catholique, plutôt qu'à une volonté soudaine de préserver la langue et la culture française en Amérique du Nord. Néanmoins, l'adoption de l'*Acte de Québec* témoignait aussi d'un respect naissant et d'une tolérance réelle à l'égard de la différence culturelle préservée par la population canadienne française, appelée désormais à vivre à l'intérieur des cadres d'une Colonie-Britannique. Fait important, l'*Acte de Québec* de 1774, en reconnaissant publiquement la culture de la population canadienne française, a alors créé un espace *public* pour la culture et les valeurs de la population française.

Après la crise provoquée par des révoltes durement réprimées en 1837-38 et une nouvelle tentative infructueuse d'assimilation après cette répression, ce même type de reconnaissance publique de la différence culturelle s'est retrouvé dans l'*Acte de l'Amérique du Nord Britannique*, adopté par le Parlement de Londres en 1867 (maintenant la *Loi constitutionnelle* de 1867), qui créait la fédération canadienne et le Canada moderne. L'article 93 de la Constitution a alors conféré aux législatures provinciales le pouvoir de décréter des lois relatives à l'éducation, mais en même temps a interdit à ces mêmes législatures de porter atteinte aux droits et privilèges conférés, lors de l'union, relativement à l'enseignement religieux. À un moment dans l'histoire où les francophones étaient pour la plupart catholiques et les anglophones pour la plupart protestants, en raison de la garantie du droit à l'enseignement confessionnel, la législature provinciale ne pouvait compromettre le droit à un enseignement catholique ou protestant de la minorité catholique de l'Ontario et de la minorité protestante du Québec. L'article 93 existe toujours aujourd'hui et s'applique encore, avec de légères modifications, dans plusieurs provinces canadiennes.

Depuis la mise en vigueur de la *Charte canadienne des droits et libertés* en 1982, le Canada a progressé encore davantage vers la reconnaissance publique et privée de la diversité culturelle au Canada. Cette *Charte* n'a pas seulement consolidé et étendu les libertés civiles traditionnelles: elle a aussi voulu reconnaître des droits culturels, parfois à caractère collectif ou communautaire.

Par exemple, l'article 16 de la *Charte* fait de l'anglais et du français les langues officielles du Canada et du Nouveau-Brunswick. L'article 20 impose au gouvernement l'obligation de fournir au public des services bilingues. L'article 23 de la *Charte* est encore plus innovateur car il constitutionnalise le droit des "citoyens canadiens"qui font partie de la minorité anglophone du Québec ou de la minorité francophone ailleurs au pays "de faire instruire leurs enfants, aux niveaux primaire et secondaire, dans la langue de la minorité [...] d'une province". Ce droit appartient aux parents et il peut faire l'objet de certaines restrictions. En effet, il "s'exerce partout dans la province où le nombre des enfants des citoyens qui ont ce droit est suffisant pour justifier à leur endroit la prestation, sur les fonds publics, de l'instruction dans la langue de la minorité" (alinéa 23(3)*a*)).

Par ailleurs, l'article 35 de la *Loi constitutionnelle de 1982* reconnaît et confirme les droits existants ancestraux ou issus de traités des peuples autochtones du Canada. L'article 35 fait maintenant l'objet d'un long et complexe contentieux constitutionnel. En effet, cette disposition a été de plus en plus invoquée par les peuples autochtones du Canada afin d'obtenir la reconnaissance publique de certains droits de chasse et de pêche ainsi que de droits plus importants, mais encore mal définis, à un titre aborigène sur une partie substantielle du territoire canadien et à des formes d'autonomie gouvernementale des Premières Nations du Canada. Fait important, la reconnaissance constitutionnelle de droits existants issus de traités implique elle-même parfois la reconnaissance d'une forme de rapport d'État à État entre la Couronne et les Premières nations. Le Canada tente maintenant de résoudre les difficultés qui résultent de ces rapports historiques. L'existence d'autres "États"à l'intérieur des frontières serait un problème très difficile à régler pour qui appartient à la tradition "républicaine"du statut de l'État. Il est à espérer que la tradition du Canada d'acceptation de la diversité permettra d'établir le fondement d'une méthode de reconnaissance des communautés autochtones et de leurs droits, à l'intérieur toutefois du cadre constitutionnel canadien.

Jusqu'ici, j'ai surtout traité de l'acceptation de la diversité culturelle par la reconnaissance des droits des minorités. Je ne veux toutefois pas suggérer que l'on peut se permettre de sous-estimer l'importance de la reconnaissance et de la protection des droits individuels. En vérité, il est essentiel pour un État qui désire reconnaître la diversité à l'intérieur de ses frontières d'accorder aux personnes un ensemble de droits qui assure à chacune d'entre elles le respect de sa valeur et de sa dignité intrinsèques en tant qu'être humain.

L'article 15 de la *Charte* canadienne et l'article 10 de la *Charte québécoise des droits et libertés de la personne* représentent deux tentatives différentes, une de la part du Canada et l'autre de la part du Québec, de protéger la dignité humaine en interdisant la discrimination injustifiée et en favorisant l'égalité. L'article 15 de la *Charte canadienne* prévoit que la loi ne fait acception de personne et s'applique également à tous, et que tous ont droit à la même protection et au même bénéfice de la loi, indépendamment de toute discrimination. Parmi les motifs interdits de discrimination énumérés à l'article 15, on retrouve la discrimination fondée sur la race, l'origine nationale ou ethnique, la couleur et la religion. Je mentionne en particulier ces motifs interdits de discrimination parce que, sur le plan individuel, la protection à l'encontre de la discrimination fondée sur la race, la religion, l'origine nationale ou ethnique représente toujours une condition essentielle à la reconnaissance de la différence culturelle sur le plan collectif. Dans une démocratie présentant des traits communautaires comme au Canada, la protection des droits individuels et culturels va de pair avec celle des droits que la collectivité peut posséder. Par exemple, afin de jouir pleinement de leurs droits en matière d'éducation en vertu de l'article 23 de la *Charte canadienne*, les minorités francophones ou anglophones des provinces doivent également être protégées contre les lois discriminatoires qui touchent d'autres aspects de leurs vies. Par ailleurs, la protection contre la discrimination dépasse l'exigence du simple traitement identique. Comme l'a souligné la Cour suprême du Canada dans *Andrews c. Law Society of British Columbia*, "toute différence de traitement entre des individus dans la loi ne produira pas forcément une inégalité et, [...] un traitement identique peut fréquemment engendrer de graves inégalités".[8]

Fait également important, on retrouve au Québec des garanties similaires à l'article 10 de la *Charte québécoise des droits et libertés de la personne*. Cette disposition prévoit que toute personne a droit à la reconnaissance et à l'exercice, en pleine égalité, des droits et libertés de la personne, sans distinction, exclusion ou préférence fondée notamment sur la race, la couleur, l'état civil, la religion, les convictions politiques, la langue, l'origine ethnique ou nationale.

La *Charte québécoise* et les lois analogues relatives aux droits de la personne adoptées par les autres provinces possèdent un "caractère fondamental et quasi-constitutionnel"[9], ce qui signifie qu'elles jouissent d'une suprématie par rapport aux autres lois. Les objectifs de la *Charte* québécoise, notamment la protection de la dignité humaine et le droit à l'égalité pour tous les êtres humains, visent implicitement, dans leur ensemble, à éliminer toute discrimination. Ces idéaux de dignité humaine, d'égalité et de protection contre la discrimination sont essentiels dans *toute* démocratie.

Jusqu'ici, j'ai insisté sur la nécessité d'appliquer un traitement *différent* à certaines collectivités et à certains groupes culturels au sein d'une démocratie. J'ai constaté qu'un modèle républicain d'intégration, c'est-à-dire le "melting pot", peut avoir pour effet de rejeter les communautés culturelles dans l'obscurité politique. Cela dit, le besoin existe toujours dans une démocratie de s'assurer que les personnes appartenant à des communautés culturelles différentes soient traitées avec le même respect et la même dignité. D'ailleurs, la reconnaissance de ces droits à l'égalité transmet également un message clair que, même en vertu d'une vision communautaire, la citoyenneté relève d'un ensemble de valeurs communes partagées par la société civile dans son ensemble. En effet, ces droits à l'égalité ont pour conséquence que lorsque, par exemple, des personnes postulent pour un emploi, lorsqu'elles demandent des allocations gouvernementales ou lorsqu'elles interagissent avec d'autres personnes dans le domaine privé, on peut affirmer qu'elles exercent leurs droits démocratiques en tant que citoyens. Ces personnes ne doivent pas alors être victimes de discrimination fondée sur les mythes et les stéréotypes liés à leurs antécédents culturels. La *reconnaissance* de la diversité dans une démocratie communautaire devient alors une valeur commune. Elle reflète un engagement commun de respect mutuel et d'acceptation de l'autre dans sa différence et son authenticité.

Les défis de la reconnaissance de la diversité

Si souhaitable que l'on estime une accommodation profonde des diversités, on ne saurait nier qu'une vision communautaire de la démocratie engendre des tensions dans la société civile, entre droits individuels et droits collectifs, entre l'individu et la communauté à laquelle il se rattache. Les droits des personnes à l'égalité et à la protection contre la discrimination doivent coexister avec certains droits collectifs de nature politique ou culturelle. Ainsi, d'une part, nous reconnaissons le droit d'une minorité linguistique à un traitement différent en matière d'instruction en donnant à ses enfants l'accès à l'instruction dans leur langue maternelle, même si elle diffère de la langue parlée par la majorité dans un territoire particulier. D'autre part, lorsque ces mêmes enfants entrent sur le marché du travail ou demandent un service public une allocation gouvernementale, le droit des libertés civiles exigera qu'elles soient traitées individuellement dans le respect des valeurs de dignité et d'égalité, pour leur ouvrir toutes les possibilités qu'offre la vie de la société civile.

Ils conservent toutefois aussi le droit au respect de cette dignité et de cette égalité à l'intérieur de leur propre communauté, dans la vie et les activités de celle-ci. La présence et l'interaction des droits individuels et des droits collectifs confirment les difficultés inhérentes à la reconnaissance de la diversité au sein d'une démocratie. Il faut reconnaître la diversité culturelle mais, à un moment donné, il reste nécessaire de partager des intérêts communs et une citoyenneté commune. Il n'est plus de cité ou de communauté politique large, lorsque ne subsistent que des îlots autonomes, protégés dans et par leur isolement. Il est justifié de se demander jusqu'à quel point un état démocratique peut pousser la reconnaissance de la diversité avant que les tensions qu'engendre celle-ci ne deviennent intolérables. Pouvons-nous préconiser l'ouverture jusqu'à permettre à des groupes d'appliquer leurs propres systèmes juridiques, indépendamment de la société plus large à laquelle ils appartiennent? Par exemple, des inquiétudes se sont manifestées récemment au Canada quant à la possibilité de permettre le recours à la charia, dans certaines provinces canadiennes, dans les procédures d'arbitrage en matière de droit de la famille. Se pose ensuite la question de l'autonomie gouvernementale des Autochtones, un domaine encore peu exploré au Canada. Comment le Canada composera-t-il avec la volonté des Premières Nations qui aspirent à une plus grande autonomie politique, tout en restant fidèle à la *Charte canadienne des droits et libertés* ainsi qu'au cadre de la constitution de notre pays et à ses valeurs constitutionnelles en général?

Une fois encore, je suggère de revenir aux idées de Charles Taylor qui a beaucoup réfléchi sur la reconnaissance de la diversité profonde au Canada et dans d'autres pays. Des tensions se manifesteront inéluctablement lorsque l'on tentera de discuter des aspects pratiques d'une vision communautaire de la démocratie. Les analyses juridiques les plus fines ou les jugements les mieux charpentés ne réussiront pas à établir des cadres juridiques ou politiques qui permettront de prévoir et de résoudre à l'avance tous les problèmes d'une reconnaissance des diversités ou d'une conciliation des diverses catégories de droits. Le Canada, ainsi que d'autres États, doivent tenter de composer avec ces tensions inévitables, pour les régler pragmatiquement, mais sans oublier leurs valeurs fondamentales. Les groupes culturels, les grands comme les petits, continueront de chercher à étendre la portée de la reconnaissance de leurs différences, et ce, tant au niveau public et collectif qu'au niveau individuel. La société doit tenir compte, d'une part, de ces diverses réclamations et, d'autre part, du besoin qu'a toute démocratie de préserver un degré suffisant de solidarité et de communauté d'intérêts. En pratique, les juges, les arbitres, les politiciens et les ombudsmans vivent quotidiennement avec cette tension et parviennent souvent à y porter remède.

Il est d'ailleurs utile de se rappeler que les droits, collectifs et individuels, ne s'exercent pas dans l'abstrait. Il existe un "horizon de signification" en fonction duquel nous apprécions tous la valeur et la validité des revendications de droits. En reconnaissant le droit d'une minorité culturelle à une autonomie accrue dans un domaine ou dans un autre, non seulement nous reconnaissons la valeur que cela représente pour la minorité en question, mais nous exprimons également une vision commune de ce que signifie le fait de constituer une société démocratique. Si nous choisissons par exemple d'établir un droit positif à l'instruction dans la langue de la minorité, nous reconnaissons que la minorité possède intrinsèquement ce droit, mais en même temps, nous prenons position à l'égard des membres de cette communauté et de leur dignité comme personnes humaines. Cette position signifie que nous voudrions être traités avec le même respect et la même dignité si un jour les rôles venaient à changer.

Lorsque les droits sont vus sous cet angle, lorsqu'ils sont rattachés à un horizon de signification que nous partageons tous, la minorité comme la majorité, la tâche parfois difficile de vivre dans la tension d'une démocratie communautaire devient plus supportable. Ironiquement (j'en ai parlé brièvement un peu plus tôt), au Canada, notre volonté de reconnaître la diversité culturelle, malgré les craintes d'effets potentiellement négatifs sur la cohésion nationale, a mené sur le plan organique à un tout nouveau type de cohésion nationale et de valeurs communes. Le Canada, si je ne m'abuse, s'est fait au-delà de ses frontières une réputation de société tolérante, pacifique, pluraliste et vivante. En refusant d'imposer un modèle homogène de citoyenneté, par le recours à un degré substantiel d'empathie et à une volonté significative de compromis, nous espérons avoir créé de nouveaux liens entre citoyens de notre pays. Je ne comprendrais pas pourquoi nous ne pourrions pas préserver et renforcer ces liens en continuant d'honorer et de respecter pendant longtemps nos différences respectives, pourvu que cette reconnaissance s'accompagne du maintien des valeurs fondamentales de liberté, d'égalité et de respect de la dignité et de l'intégrité de tous les membres de la société civile.

Conclusion générale—le rôle d'Ombudsman et de médiateur public

Jusqu'ici, je n'ai guère abordé le rôle que vous, en tant qu'ombudsmans ou médiateurs publics, pouvez jouer lorsqu'il s'agit de reconnaître la diversité culturelle dans un monde démocratique. Selon moi, le rôle d'ombudsman consiste à tenter, en quelque sorte, de passer du général au spécifique. Vous devez, dans vos activités quotidiennes, chercher à reconnaître et à comprendre d'une façon concrète les traits caractéristiques et les problèmes propres des personnes différentes aux yeux des majorités, lorsqu'elles sont confrontées à des bureaucraties gouvernementales et à des systèmes juridiques qui parfois ignorent totalement ce qu'elles sont et ce qu'elles ont vécu. Il vous fait alors à la fois découvrir et suggérer les solutions propres à leurs besoins particuliers pour faciliter leur participation à la vie commune de la société.

Dans les tâches difficiles qui sont les vôtres, j'espère que ces quelques réflexions vous auront été utiles. Dans le cadre de l'exercice de vos fonctions, la diversité culturelle et les différentes perspectives sociales qu'elle engendre ne doivent pas être perçues comme une faiblesse regrettable de la démocratie moderne, mais comme l'un de ses fondements. La reconnaissance spécifique des différences, qu'elles soient linguistiques, religieuses, culturelles ou autres, constitue une solution viable, dans la mesure où la différence qui doit faire l'objet d'une reconnaissance repose sur des valeurs capables de rejoindre l'ensemble des citoyens, c'est-à-dire tant que la reconnaissance recherchée peut être liée à un ensemble de valeurs communes qui constitue notre horizon de sens collectif. Ceci dit, il restera jour après jour à affronter les difficultés de cette identification et de cette conciliation de valeurs. Ultimement, les solutions dépendront peut-être de notre aptitude à nous placer dans la situation de ces personnes différentes, des membres de ces communautés distinctes et, au moins en imagination, à cheminer avec elles, un moment, dans la société civile qui les accueille.

Notes en fin d'ouvrage

1. Dominique Schnapper, «La République face aux communautarismes» *Études revue de culture contemporaine*, 400:2 (février 2004) 177.

2. [1983] Can. Hum. Rts. Y.B. 306 (Comité des droits de l'homme des N.-U.).

3. (1996), VI Cour, Eur. D.H. (Sér. A.), 24 E.H.R.R. 294. Voir également Clare Ovey & Robin C.A. While, Jacobs & White, *The European Convention on Human Rights*.

4. Voir *Affaire linguistique belge* (n° 1) (1967), 5 Cour Eur. D.H. (Sér. A)1 E.H.R.R. 241 et *Affair linguistique belge (N° 2)* (1968), 6 Cour Eur. D.H. (Sér. A) 1 E.H.R.R. 252 dans lesquels la Cour a décidé que l'article 2 ne comprenait pas un droit de recevoir de l'instruction dans la langue de choix des parents, ni un droit d'accès à une école particulière choisie par les parents.

5. Robert Dunbar, «Implications of the European Charter for Regional or Minority Languages for British Linguistic Minorities» (2000) 25 E.L. Rev. Human Rights Survey 46.

6. Voir, par exemple, l'article 7—Objectifs et Principes, qui demande que les États "fondent leur politique, leur législation et leur pratique sur les objectifs et principes suivants: [notamment] la mise à disposition de formes et moyens adéquats d'enseignement et d'études des langues régionales ou minoritaires à tous les stades appropriés."

7. Dominique Breillat, «La Charte européenne des langues régionales ou minoritaires: le cas français» (2001) 35 R.J.T. 697.

8. [1989] 1 R.C.S. 143.

9. *Québec (Commission des droits de la personne et des droits de la jeunesse) c. Montréal (Ville)*, [2000] 1 R.C.S. 665 au para. 27.

PROTECTING RIGHTS AND FREEDOMS

Emily O'Reilly*

Les ombudsmans font face à de nombreux nouveaux défis dans le cadre de leur travail de protection des droits et libertés individuels: entre autres, depuis les attaques contre les États-Unis, toutes les conséquences associées aux mesures prises par les gouvernements, à l'échelle mondiale, pour combattre le terrorisme et contrôler l'immigration.

On sait que ce sont les conditions juridiques locales qui définissent le rôle des ombudsmans du secteur public, mais toutes ces nouvelles pressions externes risquent de limiter la protection des droits qu'ils fournissent traditionnellement.

Cet article traite de la législation internationale sur les droits de l'Homme, et il encourage les ombudsmans à s'y intéresser, en plus des lois domestiques, pour leurs enquêtes sur les plaintes qui leur sont soumises. Le droit international repose, en effet, sur une plus grande diversité d'intérêts, et une bonne connaissance de cette législation peut permettre aux ombudsmans de se faire une idée plus juste de la situation générale des cas particuliers qu'ils ont à traiter.

****

Los ombudsmen enfrentan nuevos desafíos en su tarea de proteger los derechos y libertades individuales. Entre ellos se encuentran las implicancias de las

* Ombudsman of Ireland. This paper was presented at the VIIIth Conference of the International Ombudsman Institute in Québec City on September 9, 2004.

medidas tomadas para combatir el terrorismo después de los ataques en los Estados Unidos de América, así como también los efectos de las medidas gubernamentales mundiales a fin de controlar la inmigración El cometido del ombudsman del sector público se determina de acuerdo con el entorno legislativo doméstico. Sin embargo, nuevas presiones que provienen de fuentes externas tienen la capacidad de limitar la protección tradicionalmente brindada por el ombudsman.

Este documento destaca la importancia de la ley internacional de derechos humanos y alienta a los ombudsmen a tenerla en cuenta además de las leyes locales cuando realizan el examen de quejas. La ley internacional abarca una gama más extensa de intereses y posibilita la formación de una visión más amplia de lo que es justo y razonable en cualquier caso particular.

Introduction

If we were fortunate enough to live in a Utopian society we would expect each individual to put the common good before his or her own personal interests. We would expect to find a perfect balance between the public interest and individual interests without the need for state intervention. Unfortunately, in the real world, these interests do not lie in perfect equilibrium. Hence the need for governments, parliaments, the courts (with appropriate separation of powers), domestic and international laws, police forces, defence forces, prisons, regulatory bodies, and various types of watchdogs. Of course, subject to domestic constitutional provisions, ombudsmen have the important task of ensuring that these organs of the typical modern democratic state discharge their functions in a proper manner.

The Effects of Globalization

Up to the early 1990s, most of the then existing ombudsman offices had little difficulty in discharging their respective remits by focusing on the internal legislative regime within their own countries. The more traditional ombudsman offices were focused mainly on the concept of "maladministration"—*i.e.* the extent to which the law of the land was implemented in a proper, fair, open, and impartial manner. The newly emerging democracies bestowed on their ombudsmen a wider remit of investigating not only maladministration, but also human rights infringements. This wider remit, in many instances, was a recognition of the failure of the traditional judicial process to properly protect and enforce human rights protections within their countries.

Throughout the 1990s, new factors have emerged which have added increasing complexity to the work of ombudsmen and related institutions. Insofar as the protection of rights and freedoms is concerned, the principal developments have been:

- The globalization of commerce and, in particular, the privatization of public utilities (e.g. telecommunications, electricity, water) and, in many instances, their subsequent absorption into multinational corporations;

- The globalization of terrorism in the aftermath of the September 11, 2001 attacks in the United States of America and the implications for individual freedom and privacy; and

- The effects of immigration and the extent to which immigrants, asylum seekers, and refugees are successfully integrated into the host country.

Privatization

Public utilities were traditionally within the remit of the relevant public sector ombudsman but, in the interests of making them more responsive to the demands of the marketplace and in order to downsize public services, governments across the world have privatized many of these utilities. In order to ensure accountability, they are now generally within the remit of industry regulators. However, these regulators are principally concerned with issues of pricing and standards. Issues of consumer protection are dictated by the market rather than the concepts of fairness and equity—the traditional benchmarks used by an ombudsman in investigating complaints.

In some cases, specialist industry ombudsmen have been appointed, but these are not always fully independent of the industry. In other cases the industry may remain within the jurisdiction of the relevant public sector ombudsman. There can be difficulties for either an industry ombudsman or a public sector ombudsman in ensuring accountability of a privatized utility operating in a competitive market. The corporate governance standards of multinational companies are normally formulated in the headquarter country and are not always in harmony with the social, economic, environmental, and cultural norms of the countries in which they are located. These developments are posing new challenges for ombudsmen.

The Implications of Global Terrorism

The September 11th attacks raise two important issues. First, there is the need for enhanced security measures which are placing new restrictions on individual freedom and privacy. Second, differences have emerged between the United States (U.S.) and the European Union (EU) and its individual member states as to where the balance should lie between these competing needs.

Both of these issues are best exemplified in the agreement signed in May 2004 between the U.S. and the EU which allows for the transfer of thirty-four pieces of information about airline passengers to U.S. authorities (such as names, contact numbers, bank and credit card numbers, home and e-mail addresses, and other details which can be held for up to three and a half years). One month later, the President of the European Parliament referred the agreement to the European Court of Justice on the grounds that it inadequately reflects EU data protection legislation. The agreement was intended to modify the unilateral decision by U.S. authorities to seek such passenger information. Most European airlines agreed to do so, under the threat of fines and the possible loss of landing rights.

The Parliament's concern is that the lack of equivalent data protection and privacy rights in the U.S. will allow such information to be given to private operators. The President of the European Parliament, Mr. Pat Cox, said there was a "new kind of creeping extra-territoriality" behind the U.S. policy which should be tested by the European Court. If the EU's draft Constitutional Treaty is ratified, the Parliament's position in dealing with such issues will be strengthened.

Immigration and Integration

Immigration is now the number one public policy issue in most countries in the EU. From an ombudsman's perspective, it raises two issues. First, the ombudsman must consider the extent to which governments have devised immigration policies which are fair and reasonable and the extent to which these policies are implemented in a proper manner that is consistent with principles of good administration. Understandably, governments are looking more closely at their policies in this area in the light of international security threats. Also, measures are being devised to counter international trade in people trafficking which has led to exploitation and tragic loss of life. The second issue is the extent to which those immigrants who are legally resident in the host country are entitled to public services such as health, education, and housing.

Some EU countries operate two-tier systems whereby immigrants have lesser entitlements to state benefits. Others do not discriminate between nationals and non-nationals. Others, still, are relatively homogeneous with low levels of net immigration. Some commentators have raised concerns about the capacity of governments to accommodate diversity on the scale which we are now witnessing.[1] They make the point that diversity is placing new demands on the welfare systems of those countries that have been at the forefront in embracing immigration. In addition to the obvious problems caused by a rationing of scarce resources, surveys have shown that indigenous populations often resent the fact that benefits and entitlements are allocated equally among all applicants regardless of origin. In other words, the concept of fairness may, in fact, be far more complex than simply ensuring equal treatment for all. The issues raised by immigration have obvious implications for ombudsmen and related institutions.

New Challenges for Ombudsmen

The common factor underpinning these three issues is globalization. Freedom of movement (illegal or legal) is now possible on a scale which never could have been envisaged even fifteen years ago. It has the potential to offer unparalleled economic and social benefits. But it also carries significant threats which have already prompted many governments to curb individual rights and freedoms. It has also opened up differences in the approaches adopted by the U.S. and the EU, in particular.

The remit of the ombudsman, and the public sector ombudsman in particular, traditionally has been shaped by the domestic legislative environment which he or she inhabits. Even those ombudsmen who are concerned solely with maladministration see themselves as "pushing out the boundaries" by demanding increasingly higher standards of administration from the public authorities which they supervise. But are we witnessing new pressures from external sources which have the capacity to limit the protections traditionally offered by ombudsmen to their clients? Is a new world order of shared values beginning to emerge which is inferior to those already existing in many countries? If this is the case, what is the ombudsman's reaction to these developments?

This paper explores these issues in some detail. In particular, it looks to international human rights law and encourages all ombudsmen to have regard to it in addition to relevant domestic law when examining complaints. In view of the fact that international norms are, by definition, based on a wider community of interests, this paper suggests that ombudsmen should use these norms to form a more expansive view of what is fair and reasonable in any particular case.[2]

This broader approach to examining complaints, it is suggested, may be of assistance in dealing with issues relevant to the new international security requirements and issues relating to immigration. Difficulties arising in relation to privatization are, essentially, issues of consumer protection and are outside the scope of this paper.

Addressing the Challenges

In attempting to answer these questions, the first point to recognize is that there are variations in the capacity of different ombudsmen to address these issues.

As I stated earlier, some are concerned solely with maladministration and injustice, or adverse effect, within the confines of domestic legislation, rules, schemes, or programmes. Others have a wider role in commenting on and recommending improvements in existing legislation which, in the ombudsman's opinion, operates unfairly. Others, still, have the power to test the constitutionality of proposed legislation. Particularly in the newly emerging democracies, ombudsmen have power similar to, or overlapping with, the courts and specific remits in relation to protection of human rights.

A Hierarchy of Rights

The second point to consider in addressing these challenges is the broad background of rights against which any complaint to an ombudsman potentially might be analyzed.

The so-called first generation rights are civil and political rights. These rights are normally enforceable through the courts, but not exclusively so. Second generation rights are social, economic, and cultural rights. Because they are resource intensive, there are limits on the extent to which these rights may be enforced through the courts or through other appellate systems, and governments across the world differ in the degree to which they facilitate enforceability of these rights. Thirdly, there is the area of administrative justice—the area in which the traditional ombudsman operates.

It is important to note that maladministration can encompass human rights issues, although it is not always seen in these terms by public servants or, indeed, by ombudsmen and their staff. Ombudsman offices are often not accustomed to analyzing complaints from this wider perspective and, indeed, staff may lack the knowledge and expertise to do so. But ombudsmen and their staff do need to recognize that if the first and second generation rights are not properly or adequately protected, there may be difficulties for them in ensuring that their traditional preserve—sound and fair administration—operates in a proper manner. In essence, this means that ombudsmen should take the broadest possible view of their role and see it as encompassing two principle aims namely, promoting respect for human dignity and protecting individuals who are dependent on public authorities.

It is also the case that an ombudsman's remit may not specifically provide that he or she is obliged to examine complaints from a human rights perspective, but it is rarely the case that the office is specifically precluded from doing so. If an ombudsman is to adopt the wider approach, there are certain conditions which must be met and these are discussed later.

Many of the complaints of maladministration which are dealt with by a classical ombudsman may have human rights aspects to them. For example, my Office investigated several complaints relating to the failure of the health authorities to pay subventions that the residents of nursing homes were legally entitled to receive. Although the complaints were presented as examples of maladministration, they raised important human rights issues about the care of the elderly. Regrettably, the public authorities were unaware of this dimension of the complaints until it was brought to their attention by my Office. My predecessor, Kevin Murphy, commented as follows in his investigation report:

> With the passing of the *Human Right Commission Act*, 2000 and the intention that the European Convention on Human Rights will become part of Irish law, it is clear that international human rights instruments will increasingly represent a significant influence in the State's approach to service provision. This is likely to be particularly so in the case of entitlements for groups such as children, the disabled, the homeless, travellers and other minority groups, the elderly, immigrants and persons in custody and detention. A human rights approach may not, in fact, be all that different to what our Constitution already provides; but it may well be the catalyst to unlocking what is already contained in the Constitution. This approach will pose fresh challenges for our institutions of government.....[They] will have to develop an awareness of the relevance of human rights protection not only to existing international instruments but also to domestic law and, indeed, to administrative schemes and programmes which are not part of domestic law.[3]

The Courts, Human Rights Commissions, and the Ombudsman

Before exploring further the ombudsman's capacity to have regard to international human rights norms, it is worth asking whether he or she has a role to play in this area or whether indeed, this approach should be left to the courts (domestic and international) or, if one exists, the human rights commission of the country in question.

In general terms, the courts are concerned with legality and will base their decisions on the written law. The ombudsman, too, has regard to legality but also to fairness and reasonableness as derived from principles of good administration. To illustrate what this means in practice, many of you will be aware that my Office published a guide to standards of best practice for public servants. The guide advises public servants, in their dealings with the public, to operate in a proper, fair, open, and impartial manner and gives examples of best practice which achieves these aims.

The courts are concentrated on achieving redress for the plaintiff and are generally unconcerned about improving systems and procedures. By contrast, the latter area is of major concern to the ombudsman.

Human Rights Commissions (HRCs) cover the public and private sectors and have a strong advocacy and promotional role as well as an investigatory role. However, where a complaint is made to a HRC about a matter which is within the jurisdiction of another investigatory body (*i.e.* the ombudsman), it is usual to refer it to that office for investigation.

Some HRCs have complained about inadequate state funding and clearly this can have implications for their effectiveness. For example, the Council of Europe Commissioner for Human Rights, Mr. Alvaro Gil-Robles, commenting on the Northern Ireland Human Rights Commission, stated:

> The (Northern Ireland Human Rights) Commission noted that it had not been as effective as it might have been because of the lack of resources available to it and listed in its report a number of activities that had therefore been curtailed. The Commission's current ordinary budget barely covers basic staffing and accommodation costs, leaving little for its actual activities. The Commission is consequently obliged to submit additional bids during the budget year for further resources in order to carry out specific tasks related to its mandate. Under this system the Secretary of State for Northern Ireland, to whom such bids are made, is unduly able to influence the autonomy, and hence the independence, of the Commission. A clear statement on the need for sufficient resources and on the principle of financial autonomy would address these concerns.[4]

Coincidentally, the Human Rights Commission of the Republic of Ireland which, in common with the Northern Ireland HRC, was established under the Good Friday Agreement of 1998, has also complained about inadequate funding.[5]

Some ombudsman offices, notably in South America and Eastern Europe, combine the functions of a HRC. Other countries which have not had a stable democracy and rule of law have given their ombudsmen a specific role in the protection of human rights. A number of countries have an ombudsman for children or a commissioner for children to address specific human rights concerns insofar as they relate to children.

It is clear from the above that despite the excellent work done by formal judicial systems and HRCs in the protection of human rights, there are opportunities for ombudsmen to complement the work of these agencies, and thus render more complete protection afforded to individuals against infringements.

Domestic Law and/or International Human Rights Law?

If, when investigating complaints, an ombudsman is to have regard to international human rights law, there are certain conditions which must be satisfied.

First, there is the question of whether international law is part of domestic law within the state or whether there are arrangements in place to incorporate it by means of domestic statute. In some countries the constitution provides for the domestic application of international treaty obligations whereas in others, these obligations do not automatically become part of the domestic legal system. Instead, a separate statute is required to act as the legal source of rights within the state.

Second, there is the question of whether the ombudsman has an express human rights mandate or whether he or she is limited to investigating administrative actions. Even if the ombudsman does not have a specific human rights mandate, he or she is not precluded from calling upon such norms provided, of course, the state, either automatically or by domestic legislation, has given effect to international obligations. Even if the state has not given effect domestically to international obligations, the ombudsman can still use these norms as a guide to a more informed view of what constitutes fairness and equity. These approaches are discussed in more detail in the final section of this paper.

Commentators are divided on the question of whether it is at all appropriate for an ombudsman to have regard to international norms. Some have taken the view that domestic law is the principal support for the ombudsman with international standards being, at most, of indirect relevance.[6] The Danish Parliamentary Ombudsman, Hans Gammeltoft-Hansen, takes a different view:

> Since the Ombudsman, from a general point of view, is always concerned with the protection of the individual citizen against some part of the apparatus of the state, it is quite obvious and adequate that the Ombudsman could make use of human rights standards binding the Danish state—and in many respects elaborated by the human rights organs (especially, of course, the organs connected to the European Convention of Human Rights) through the so-called dynamic interpretation.[7]

The former National Ombudsman of the Netherlands, Dr. Martin Oosting, takes a similar view and the work of his Office in the human rights area is described later in this paper.[8]

Also, in newly developing countries there may be a need to look to international norms and this is already recognized in some African states.

But global security and global immigration issues are forcing governments to enter into international co-operation arrangements to deal with these new pressures. There are concerns about the degree to which parliaments and the public are generally informed about: what may be agreed in their name and the extent to which individual freedom may be compromised in the interests of worldwide security.

In this rapidly changing environment, international human rights treaties and conventions—precisely because of their international status—have a new relevance in safeguarding existing rights and, where relevant, should be taken into account by ombudsmen in their examination of complaints.

Some Examples of the Threats to Individual Rights and Freedoms

Security and Human Rights

In the aftermath of the September 11th atrocities, the U.S. and the EU initiated discussions in relation to the introduction of a wide range of security measures to combat terrorism. It is not the function of this paper to evaluate the merits of these measures, or in any sense to question their necessity. Rather, the purpose is to show how, in the light of these unprecedented events, the measures may impact on individual rights and freedoms.

The first three agreements negotiated between the U.S. and the EU were the Europol-USA Agreement, EU-USA Judicial Co-operation Agreement, and the agreement between the European Commission and the U.S. Department of Homeland Security in relation to passenger names records. The latter agreement was described in some detail in the opening paragraphs of this paper. There was criticism, at the time, of the culture of secrecy and the resistance to parliamentary scrutiny which surrounded the negotiations.

An agreement on the exchange of police data was concluded in November 2002. Because of preexisting EU directives, the agreement raised data protection difficulties on the EU side but not on the U.S. side, which has a less structured approach to data protection.

Negotiations on an agreement on extradition and other issues commenced in April 2002. Paul Gillespie, Foreign Editor of the Irish Times commented:

> The negotiations continued in secret over the next year, with the draft text of the agreements remaining confidential. Notwithstanding the conviction of governments that such secrecy prevented political interference from slowing co-operation, it led to a strong reaction from several national parliaments, notably in the House of Lords in Britain, which refused to accept government arguments that fighting terrorism must take priority over open democratic scrutiny of the agreements.[9]

The agreement was concluded in June 2003 and supplements existing bilateral arrangements between the U.S. and individual EU member states. In signing the agreement, both sides emphasized the need to fight terrorism and organized crime, and the mutual trust and common values shared by the EU and the U.S.

The negotiation of these agreements illustrates the challenges now faced by governments in trying to strike a balance between concerns about security and protection of human rights. Specifically, in the U.S.-EU context, it brings into focus two differing ideologies—the U.S. which sees the measures as necessary to combat the "war on terrorism" and the EU approach which, probably because of its experience in this area, is aimed at understanding the root causes of terrorism and, within that context, fine-tuning existing legal frameworks.

Clearly, concern about these issues among the EU citizenry runs very deep. In the recent elections to the European Parliament, governments which supported the U.S. position on the war in Iraq fared badly. Madrid was the target of a terrorist attack on March 11, 2004 and the outgoing Spanish government was defeated in a general election because of its support for the U.S. position on the war in Iraq.

Further evidence of EU public opinion comes from a Eurobarometer survey conducted in the fifteen EU member states in August 2003. It shows a negative evaluation of the role of the U.S. in relation to the following issues:

- growth of the world economy;
- fight against poverty in the world;
- protection of the environment; and
- peace in the world.

In relation to the fight against terrorism, the U.S. received a positive evaluation of just six percentage points. However, there were wide variations among individual member states ranging from a positive rating of thirty-four points to a negative rating of sixty-four points.

Immigration

In recent years, immigration has been a priority public policy issue in most EU member states. Since the September 11th atrocities, it has been given a new impetus because of the potential threats it poses to international security. International trade in people trafficking is also a major concern.

I am one of the very few—if not the only—national ombudsmen in the world whose remit specifically excludes me from investigating complaints relating to asylum and naturalization. Accordingly, I am somewhat at a disadvantage in describing my country's experience in this area from an ombudsman's perspective.

34

However, I would like to comment on the referendum on citizenship which was held in Ireland in June 2004. I am an *ex officio* member of the Referendum Commission—an independent body which conducts a public information campaign and encourages the electorate to vote.

As a result of the Good Friday Agreement of 1998, the Irish Constitution was amended and gave a constitutional right to everyone born in the island of Ireland to be a citizen of Ireland. The Irish Government became concerned that this right was being abused and that it had given rise to an increase in "citizenship tourism". It claimed that non-national women, in the late stages of pregnancy, were arriving in Ireland and having their babies in Irish maternity hospitals for the sole purpose of securing for their child the right to Irish citizenship (and, in turn, EU citizenship, where appropriate).

The Government proposed to change the Constitution so that people born in the island of Ireland would no longer have a constitutional right to be Irish citizens, unless, at the time of their birth, one of their parents is an Irish citizen or is entitled to be an Irish citizen. It also proposed that the *Oireachtas* (Parliament) would pass legislation which would govern how other people born in Ireland might become Irish citizens.

The referendum was carried by a large majority—eighty percent voted in favour. Some opponents of the proposal argued that it would create a two-tier society—*i.e.* those who, by virtue of holding citizenship, would be entitled to additional rights and benefits and those who, although living and working in Ireland, would be denied similar rights by virtue of not being citizens. Other commentators expressed disquiet that the large majority in favour of the restrictions on citizenship was influenced by a wider view that there were insufficient controls on the number of non-nationals entering Ireland, rather than by the technical merits of the Government's citizenship proposal.

This, in turn, raises wider questions—and not just in Ireland—about the capacity of governments to successfully integrate non-nationals and to allocate to them health, education, housing, and other benefits on a fair and equitable basis. For example, according to a recent Mori poll, fifty-six percent of people now believe there are too many immigrants in Britain. Yet, only nine percent of British residents are from ethnic minorities whereas the corresponding figure for the U.S. is thirty percent.

By contrast, the Nordic countries are among the most socially and ethnically homogeneous states, but they also have the most highly developed welfare policies. The U.S. has a highly diversified society but is characterized as having a weak welfare state. Some commentators have argued that there is a direct link between the degree of diversity in a state and the strength of its welfare system, not only because of the resources required to implement effective integration policies, but also because of the degree to which the indigenous population is prepared to tolerate the extension of benefits to non-nationals in an increasingly diverse society.[10]

Clearly, these issues will pose new challenges for the new EU as an entity of twenty-five member states and, indeed, for each of the constituent states which, as members of the Union, will become more attractive hosts to immigrants from third countries. There will be new challenges for ombudsmen, too, in investigating complaints. The traditional approaches to the concepts of fairness and equity may work very well in a relatively homogeneous society, but there may be different perceptions about these issues among indigenous populations in an increasingly diverse society. In this more complex environment, ombudsmen may find it useful to be guided by international human rights norms rather than solely by the tenets of domestic legislation.

The Ombudsman and Human Rights Complaints

A number of ombudsman offices have regard, to a greater or lesser extent, to international human rights law in their investigation of complaints. Among these are some of the offices in Latin America and in the African states. Of the more well established offices, the National Ombudsman of the Netherlands has developed a structured approach, particularly in relation to the International Covenant on Civil and Political Rights and the European Convention on Human Rights. The Dutch Office has jurisdiction over the police and there are several documented examples of instances where it has looked to human rights law in relation to this area and, indeed, to other areas of its brief. It should also be noted that the ombudsman legislation allows that office to have regard to international human rights obligations when investigating complaints.

Among the issues reviewed by the Dutch Office in the light of international human rights law are the deprivation of liberty, inviolability of the person (use of handcuffs, body and clothing searches, and use of force), protection of privacy (the release of information to third parties, the right to respect for the home, and the operation of the security and intelligence services), the presumption of innocence, treatment in police cells, the principle of equality and the ban on discrimination, admission of immigrants, voting rights, the right to demonstrate, the privacy of correspondence, and the right to ownership of property.

In this regard the Dutch Office is a particularly good example of an ombudman's office which uses international human rights law both imaginatively and effectively.

The Application of International Human Rights Law—The Way Forward

In countries which have become bound by international human rights law, it is necessary to determine whether it is considered to be part of domestic law. It may be that the international law is automatically part of domestic law or that this is effected through the passage of domestic enabling legislation. If either is the case the ombudsman can then rely on the domestic legal framework in investigating

36

complaints and in making recommendations. He or she can adopt this approach whether or not the office has a specific remit to investigate human rights issues.

The former National Ombudsman of the Netherlands, Dr Martin Oosting, commented that these international obligations can also be used to support more fundamental legal principles such as the obligation that government action should respect human dignity:

> Viewed in this way, there are certain situations for which the conventions [the International Covenant on Civil and Political Rights and the European Convention on Human Rights] codify fundamental principles which, as general legal principles, have a broader scope than the particular situations to which the conventions relate. The relevant provisions of the conventions are an elaboration of these principles and are, therefore, also a striking confirmation of the latter. Their special significance lies in the fact that they embody legal norms for situations in which human freedom, especially in relation to the state, is involved in a manner which has a fundamental bearing on the quality of life.[11]

In the case of countries where international obligations are not part of domestic law and have not been enacted into domestic law, the ombudsman may be able to rely on the international obligations as an interpretative guide to existing domestic human rights law. Alternatively, he or she may be able to point to the gap between the international obligations of the state and the existing domestic legislation, and illustrate how this has operated to the detriment of an individual complainant.

Finally, regardless of whether the state has formal international obligations or whether an existing international obligation forms part of domestic legislation, the ombudsman may find it helpful to use international human rights norms as an informal source of principles of fairness and equity. The benefit of this approach is that it allows the ombudsman to take a more expansive view of what is fair and reasonable, even though the particular action which is the subject of a complaint may not, in fact, contravene domestic law. By definition, international norms reflect a wider community of views as to what constitutes humane and fair conduct.

Many ombudsmen are already legally empowered to proceed in the manner outlined above. Indeed, the Ombudsman of Norway was recently granted an express human rights mandate. For those who are not, I hope that the issues I have raised will provide a basis for reflection on the relevance and effectiveness of their remits in a rapidly changing world order. For those who feel constrained to operate solely by reference to the domestic legal environment, I would exhort them to take a more expansive view of their jurisdiction along the lines which I have outlined in the previous paragraph. It seems to me that this approach is one which is open to all ombudsmen, regardless of the legal environment in which they operate. I strongly encourage them to make it part of their investigation tool-kit. Insofar as my colleague ombudsmen in Europe are concerned, there may be scope to explore these ideas further in our biennial round table meetings with the organs of the Council of Europe.

Endnotes

1.   David Goodhart, "Too Diverse?" *Prospect Magazine* 95 (February 2004).

2.   At this point I would like to pay tribute to the excellent work already done by Linda Reif of the University of Alberta in exploring these concepts. I have found her pioneering work in this area of great assistance in developing the theme of this paper. See Linda C. Reif, "The Promotion of International Human Rights Law by the Office of the Ombudsman" in Linda C. Reif ed., *The International Ombudsman Anthology: Selected Writings From The International Ombudsman Institute* (Boston: Kluwer Law International, 1999) at 271.

3.   Office of the Ombudsman, *An Investigation by the Ombudsman of Complaints Regarding Payment of Nursing Home Subventions by Health Boards* (Dublin: Office of the Ombudsman 2001) at 72.

4.   Council of Europe, Office of the Commissioner for Human Rights, *Opinion 2/2002 of the Commissioner for Human Rights, Mr. Alvaro Gil-Robles, on Certain Aspects of the Review of Powers of the Northern Ireland Human Rights Commission*, (2002) Comm. Eur. D.H. D.R. 16.

5.   Ireland, Human Rights Commission, *Report to the Government Under Section 24 of the Human Rights Commission Act* (Dublin: Irish Human Rights Commission, 2003).

6.   Brian Burdekin, "Human Rights Commissions" in J. Hatchard ed., *National Human Rights Institutions in the Commonwealth* (London: Commonwealth Secretariat, 1992).

7.   Hans Gammeltoft-Hansen, "Human Rights and The National Ombudsman" in L.A. Rehof and C. Gulmann eds., *Human Rights in Domestic Law and Development Assistance Policies of the Nordic Countries* (Dordrecht: Martinus Nijhoff Publishers, 1989) 187 at 188-189 in Reif, "The Promotion of International Human Rights Law by the Office of the Ombudsman", *supra* note 2 at 274-275.

8.   Marten Oosting, "The National Ombudsman of the Netherlands and Human Rights" in *The International Ombudsman Anthology: Selected Writings from the International Ombudsman Institute supra* note 2 at 317.

9.   Paul Gillespie, "Striking a Balance Between Security and Human Rights" inJ. Carroll and J. Travers eds., *An Indispensable Partnership: EU-U.S. Relations from an Irish Perspective* (Dublin: Institute of European Affairs, 2004) at 97.

10.   *Supra* note 1.

11.   Marten Oosting, "The Ombudsman and Human Rights Observations Based on the Experience of the National Ombudsman of the Netherlands", *Occasional Paper 46* (Edmonton, International Ombudsman Institute, February 1992), in Reif, "The Promotion of Human Rights Law by the Office of the Ombudsman", *supra* note 2 at 282.

Bibliography

Birkenshaw, Patrick. *Grievances, Remedies and the State*, 2d ed. (London: Sweet & Maxwell, 1994).

Burdekin, Brian. "Human Rights Commissions" in John Hatchard ed. *National Human Rights Institutions in the Commonwealth* (London: Commonwealth Secretariat, 1992).

Council of Europe. Office of the Commissioner for Human Rights, *Opinion2/2002 of the Commissioner for Human Rights*, Mr. Avaro Gil-Robles on *Certain Aspects of the Review of the Powers of the Northern Ireland Human Rights Commission*, (2002) Comm. Eur. D.H.D.R. 16.

Gillespie, Paul. "Striking a Balance between Security and Human Rights" in Joe Carroll and John Travers eds. *An Indispensable Partnership: EU-U.S. Relations from an Irish Perspective*, (Dublin: Institute of European Affairs, 2004).

Goodhart, David. "Too Diverse?" *Prospect Magazine* 95 (February 2004).

Gregory, Roy and Philip Giddings. *Righting Wrongs: The Ombudsman in Six Continents* (Oxford: IOS Press, 2000).

Ireland, Human Rights Commission, *Report to the Government under Section 24 of the Human Rights Commission Act* (Dublin: Irish Human Rights Commission, 2003).

Jacoby, Daniel. "The Future of the Ombudsman" in Linda C. Reif ed. *The International Ombudsman Anthology: Selected Writings from the International Ombudsman Institute* (Boston: Kluwer Law International, 1999) 15.

National Economic and Social Council. *An Investment in Quality: Services, Inclusion and Enterprise* (Dublin: Government Publications, 2003).

Office of the Ombudsman. *An Investigation by the Ombudsman of Complaints Regarding Payment of Nursing Home Subventions by Health Boards* (Dublin: Office of the Ombudsman, 2001).

Office of the Ombudsman. *2002 Annual Report* (Dublin: Government Publications, 2003).

Oosting, Marten. "The National Ombudsman of the Netherlands and Human Rights" in Linda C. Reif ed. *The International Ombudsman Anthology: Selected Writings from the International Ombudsman Institute* (Boston: Kluwer Law International, 1999) 317.

Owen, Stephen. "The Ombudsman: Essential Elements and Common Challenges" in Linda C. Reif ed. *The International Ombudsman Anthology: Selected Writings from the International Ombudsman Institute* (Boston: Kluwer Law International, 1999) 51.

Referendum Commission. *The Referendum on Irish Citizenship* (Dublin: Referendum Commission, 2004).

Reif, Linda C. "The Promotion of International Human Rights Law by the Office of the Ombudsman" in Linda C. Reif ed. *The International Ombudsman Anthology: Selected Writings from the International Ombudsman Institute* (Boston: Kluwer Law International, 1999) 271.

Riordan, Patrick. "New Prospects for Citizenship: Civil Society and Civic Republicanism" (2003/4) 51 *Administration* 47.

Sinnott, Richard. "The European and Irish Public Opinion Environnent" in Joe Carroll and John Travers eds. *An Indispensable Partnership: EU-US. Relations from an Irish Perspective* (Dublin: Institute of European Affairs, 2004).

Spinosa, Charles, Fernando Flores and Hubert L. Dreyfus. *Disclosing New Worlds: Entrepreneurship, Democratic Action, and the Cultivation of Solidarity* (Cambridge: MIT Press, 1997).

Tonra, Ben. "Transatlantic Security Relations: An Irish Contribution" in Joe Carroll and John Travers eds. *An Indispensable Partnership: EU-U.S. Relations from an Irish Perspective* (Dublin: Institute of European Affairs, 2004).

THE OMBUDSMAN—MEETING TODAY'S CHANGING NEEDS

Kerstin André*

Nous devons accepter les changements et les défis, pour survivre, nous devons faire preuve de flexibilité et d'adaptation. Mais, dans notre désir de nous adapter aux circonstances, nous ne devons pas oublier la signification de notre fonction d'ombudsman: notre rôle est de promouvoir la bonne gouvernance et de protéger les droits humains fondamentaux.

Voici donc la question que nous devons nous poser: En tant qu'ombudsmans et défenseurs des droits humains fondamentaux, comment pouvons-nous répondre, de la manière la plus flexible possible, à des besoins en constante évolution, tout en maintenant notre accessibilité, notre crédibilité et notre indépendance, et en travaillant à la promotion et au respect des principes de primauté du droit et de bonne gouvernance?

****

Es cierto que debemos estar dispuestos a los cambios y a afrontar los desafíos. Si queremos sobrevivir, tenemos que ser flexibles y adaptarnos. Por el otro lado, no debemos olvidar, en nuestro entusiasmo por adaptarnos a las circunstancias, el significado del papel de ombudsmen que estamos desempeñando como supervisores del gobierno público y guardianes de los derechos humanos fundamentales.

* Kerstin André is a Parliamentary Ombudsman for Sweden. This paper was presented at the VIIIth Conference of the International Ombudsman Institute in Québec City, September 7-10, 2004.

Por consiguiente, tenemos que preguntarnos como ombudsmen y guardianes de los derechos humanos fundamentales, cómo podemos, de manera flexible, estar a la altura de las necesidades que van cambiando y, mientras conservamos nuestra accesibilidad, credibilidad e independencia, cómo podemos preservar y controlar el cumplimiento de los principios del imperio de la ley y de la buena gobernabilidad pública.

A Brief Historical Review: The Importance of Flexibility

Eight years ago, at the International Ombudman Institute Conference in Buenos Aires, four crucial criteria were laid down in order to denote an ombudsman institution: accessibility, credibility, flexibility and, not least, independence. Flexibility is the concept that I have chosen as the basis or cornerstone of some reflections in this paper. We must keep in mind that the criteria mentioned are, more or less, communicating vessels. Accordingly, what we have to ask ourselves is: how can we, as ombudsmen and guardians of fundamental human rights, in a flexible way meet today's changing needs and, at the same time, in maintaining our accessibility, credibility, and independence, preserve and monitor adherence to the principles of the rule of law and good public governance?

Times change, we know that for sure. Governments change. The tasks of public agencies change and so do the methods of fulfilling these tasks. The sociopolitical and economic surroundings change; no country today is the same as it was 100 years ago or perhaps even ten years ago. So there are, on many levels and in many aspects, continuously new conditions for the ombudsmen to face. In this context it is important to remember that an ombudsman institution established in a certain public society and during a certain period of time must not be so tied up by the existing social and legal system that it cannot meet and survive changes. I think I can state as a fact that there has always been and will always be cause to raise the same question—how to meet today's changing needs and how to respond to the new influences in order to meet the future.

As a Parliamentary Ombudsman of Sweden I represent an office of ombudsman that has existed for almost 200 years. The office is still functioning and the health conditions of the office are on the whole very good. Of course I do not want to stand out as a boaster, but I must admit that our office has so far proved to be successful in its flexible adaptation, from time to time, to the surroundings in our public society. As you can imagine, the daily work of the first Parliamentary, Ombudsman in the beginning of the nineteenth century was different from our work today. The volume of public administration and the number of public authorities to be supervised have increased immensely, and so has the number of complaints. Most cases in the old days were, as a matter of fact, initiated by the Ombudsman himself. What has changed the methods of working is, of course, the gradual development of advanced technology. Today we are not using horses when travelling round the country on inspections as were the regular means of conveyance at that time.

Also, the approach to the work has changed. Initially, the role of the original Ombudsman was greatly influenced by the power of prosecution. At that time, at the beginning of the nineteenth century, there was no idea of fulfilling the supervisory task in any other way than by concluding an investigation with a decision whether to prosecute or not; there was nothing between these alternatives. This way of acting was easy to fit in the public society at the time. Very soon, however, the ombudsman realized the need for other remedies such as admonitions, cautions, and other critical statements. This new and additional way of performing the work was accepted and further developed by his successors and also accepted by the mandator, the Parliament.

Thus, gradually, the approach to the task changed. Although the Parliamentary Ombudsmen (since 1976 there are four), as the heirs of the original ombudsman still have the power to prosecute negligent officials, today this is regarded as the ultimate weapon in the work of fulfilling our supervisory task, rather than part of our role as ombudsman. Nowadays, one of our most important tasks is to promote, through our decisions, good administrative and judicial behaviour. In other words, the approach to our task is no longer foremost repressive but constructive, educative, and preventive. Also, the recognition of human rights, although an important feature of the Ombudsman's work from the very beginning, has obtained a more predominant status. Thus it is now prescribed in the law that it is a particular duty for the Ombudsmen to ensure that the fundamental rights and freedoms of the citizens are not encroached upon in the process of public administration.

It goes without saying that the changes we have seen are connected with, and are a result of, the very fast development of public society itself. Looking closer you will realize that, although this development to some extent has affected the role of the Parliamentary Ombudsmen, far more the development has influenced the methods of working in order to fulfil the role. It is amazing that today the tasks entrusted to the Parliamentary Ombudsmen in Sweden are, on the whole, the same as in 1809 when the office was established in conjunction with the adoption of a new constitution of which it formed part. It is an interesting fact that in the middle of the 1970s, when a new instrument of government came into force, there was no need to make any fundamental changes in the basic rules of the Parliamentary Ombudsmen. Our institution had managed, within the framework of these rules, to gradually adapt to the demands of contemporary public society.

Flexibility in the International Perspective: Some General Remarks

An ombudsman institution, as every institution or public agency, can function only in its proper context. In the international perspective this is particularly evident. Although the basic idea of a supervisory institution, independent of government, is the same, it is obvious that the reality that ombudsmen meet throughout the world is different indeed. It is a demanding task and a challenge for each country to find the model ombudsman institution that is most suitable for that country under predominant circumstances. This is of course also true when choosing what methods of working are the most effective.

Apart from the constitutional differences and different legal traditions in our countries, it is only natural that the old, so-called classic ombudsman institutions, are working in a different way compared to newly established institutions in young democracies. In the old democracies, generally speaking, the fundamental base for ombudsman work has probably, in the course of time, grown more stable. In Sweden, for instance, although we must not forget about the problems that we have to face in our public administration, the principle of the rule of law has been taken for granted since medieval times. We have had courts of law and administrative authorities of a fairly modern type since the seventeenth century and, from the same period, a tradition of fairly good public administration and, later on, transparency in administrative work. We have public administrative courts of law and public decisions regarding the rights and duties of individuals can be appealed to these courts. We have a modern act of administrative procedure. We have well-functioning regular supervisory boards or agencies within almost all sectors of society. And we have a sense, passed on by heredity, for fundamental human rights.

These almost idyllic prerequisites for the ombudsman's work can be found more or less in many countries, but unfortunately not in all. It is no secret that there are still countries facing immense problems: countries where not even the judiciary functions in a satisfactory way, and countries having corruption within the public administration as the overriding problem. It is easy to realize that an ombudsman under such circumstances must have a somewhat different approach to his or her work than that of an ombudsman of the classic model, although the task is the same. And, no doubt, ombudsmen are needed in both environments. It is obvious that the idea in itself of ombudsmen has proved capable of responding to the demand of flexibility; thus the idea has proved to be very vigorous and it has an evident ability of taking root in spite of all the differences in the soil conditions.

Meeting Today's Changing Needs?

In order to meet today's changing needs we must, of course, first of all define what are today's changing needs? This question is a true challenge to answer. I am not even going to try. The answer, of course, depends on the current conditions of each country and of each ombudsman office. For the moment I will just point out, on a very general level, some of the trends that I can observe from my own horizon, trends that we have to consider in one way or another in our work as ombudsmen.

First I want to make some general remarks and even raise a flag of warning. We must indeed be open to changes and challenges. Flexiblity and adaption are necessary if we want to survive. In order to meet today's changing needs, whatever they are, there is however, speaking from the classic ombudsman point of view, no obvious need for the time being to change the ombudsman concept in itself. It is certainly not wise to allow it to answer, like a weathercock, to any change in the wind. And here again I allow myself to refer to the Swedish experience. The challenge is to adapt the ombudsman activities from time to time in order to fulfil the supervisory task in the best possible way. Of course the *modus operandi* of each ombudsman's work greatly depends on the context in which the work is performed. This discussion must be kept alive all the time. What is important is that we, in our eagerness to adapt to the circumstances, must not forget about the significance of the role that we as ombudsmen are playing as supervisors of public governance and as guardians of fundamental human rights.

From the Legalistic Public Society to the Modern Welfare State

Changes of a public society, irrespective of what public society we are talking about, may have an impact on the legal system and consequently on the environment in which the ombudsman is acting, as the legal framework is the base for his or her work. However, as many laws nowadays, not only in Sweden, are not very detailed but should be regarded more as guidelines, it is hard to say whether the application of the law is right or wrong. The result is that the scope for evaluating fairness and propriety in the actions of the authorities today is much wider than before. What is, for instance, "good quality" or "good care" in determining what is "right or wrong" in the application of a Social Welfare Act? Thus, the basis for formulating a judgement is often discretionary and not based on detailed rules. Consequently, the concept "legality" is nowadays understood in broad terms, also embracing notions such as equity, fairness, and good governance.

Supervision based on specific rules in the legal system is of course more strict than supervision based on legislation of what can be called the guideline type. Thus, the transformation from the state governed by law to the modern welfare state has, at least in some public sectors, continuously created new prerequisites for the ombudsmen (and parenthetically for the courts of law). The most important task today, also for a so-called classic ombudsman, is to promote good administrative and judicial behaviour, not *only* strictly with regard to laws and other statutes but *also* with regard to what is considered to be fair and appropriate.

This change in the approach to ombudsman work is not at all new. It has been an ongoing trend for quite a long time. I think that many, or perhaps most, of the recently established ombudsman institutions have not even experienced this development in their own work since the development has already passed. Still, I wanted to mention this briefly as it is a good example of a necessary adaption to new conditions.

Privatization of Public Service

Public power shall be exercised under law, and democracy must go hand in hand with control and supervision of public power: this is an old truth. If there is no supervision it inevitably leads to negligence or, even worse, abuse of public power and public means. Furthermore, good public governance cannot exist if the exercise of power is not combined with accountability. The supervision of public power shall lead to legality and effectiveness but also create confidence of the citizens. A society can only partially benefit from legality and effectiveness in the work of the public authorities if the citizens have no confidence in these authorities. A cornerstone in this context is openness and transparency.

The principles of the rule of law and the legal rights of individuals are very much based on the presumption that public administration will be carried out by public agencies, bound by rules in the constitution and acts of public law. Adherence to these rules is of utmost importance in order to guarantee the rights of individuals. This means, among other things, that the officials in their work are to respect the equality of each individual before the law and maintain objectivity and impartiality. Adherence to these rules is combined with accountability and parliamentary control through the ombudsmen.

Today, public service is increasingly performed by private associations. Sometimes there is even a mixture in the sense that private companies are owned fully or partially by the state or a municipality. Generally, the mandate of the parliamentary ombudsmen is linked to the principle of the rule of law within *public* administration. So one important question is how privatization of public service affects the role of the ombudsmen and, consequently, the frames of the parliamentary control, especially as the borderline between public service and public power is sometimes not very distinct.

In Sweden the constitution states that public administrative functions may be handed over to private companies or other private associations. If, however, such a function comprises exercise of public authority, it could be handed over only if it is explicitly permitted through an act of law. The problem is that there are many definitions of the concept "public administrative function". It is even more complicated to define whether such a function involves or is connected with public authority. I will not waste time by going into detail regarding this issue but only conclude that the borderlines are not easily drawn.

To meet this development, the area of competence of the Ombudsmen in Sweden has been enlarged to some extent by law. There are rules saying that if a private company is entitled by an act of law to perform public authority, this company is, in this specific context, under the supervision of the Ombudsmen. Another example is that municipal companies, when handling official public documents, are submitted to the same rules as are the public agencies and, consequently, under the supervision of the Ombudsmen. The Ombudsman's supervisory task does not only include public agencies and their employees but everyone who holds an office including exercise of public power.

As long as public service is attached to public power, we will probably keep our role unchanged when it comes to that part. Yet, a consequence of the privatization of the traditionally public administration is that the area of ambit of the Ombudsmen will gradually diminish and more and more of what is now public administration will be withdrawn from parliamentary control. It is not a question for the Ombudsmen to discuss whether the trend towards privatization of the public sector is good or not; this is a political issue. But in our role as guardians of the adherence to certain fundamental principles linked to the concept of democracy, we must be aware of the consequences and may act as watchdogs in order not to lose important features of the public administration, features very much connected with democracy itself. How can a loss of these features be compensated and what are the effects of privatization of public service in terms of protection of the legal rights of individuals?

It is worth mentioning in this context that we have faced, at least in some public sectors, changes in the ombudsman supervisory work in the sense that part of the work is nowadays directed into a control of the supervisory work performed by the regular supervisory boards and agencies. For instance, in the social welfare sector, in the medical health sector, and in the educational system a great deal of ombudsman supervision is not direct but indirect. It is not within the area of responsibility of the Parliamentary Ombudsmen to supervise private schools, private hospitals, or private nursery homes. Parliamentary control can be exercised in these sectors only indirectly by ensuring that the regular governmental authorities in their respective sector are fulfilling their supervisory task regarding the control of private subjects.

A Displacement in the Area of Responsibility

The role of the Parliamentary Ombudsmen as supervisors cannot, by the way, be looked upon in isolation from supervision within the regular system. There must be some kind of interplay between the extraordinary supervision performed by the Ombudsmen and the supervision performed by the regular authorities entrusted with supervisory power. The borderline may change due to the fact that some of these regular agencies, as I have already mentioned, also supervise some private subjects that the Parliamentary Ombudsmen do not, other than indirectly.

Public Power and Civil Law: A Mixture?

The state sometimes plays a double role: the traditional role according to the constitution and public law but, also the role of a private subject where the base for acting is civil law. There is a trend of shifting from the public sphere to the private one in the sense that the means of control of the government are displaced from the traditional ones such as laws and other regulations to civil agreements. This may lead to reflections on issues related to the constitutional difference between the role of the state as a civil agreement partner, on the one hand, and the traditional role of the state as producer of laws and regulations, and as executor of public authority according to the principle of the rule of law on the other hand.

The trend towards using civil agreements instead of regulations may be a good development in many ways, but we must be aware of this gradual change in the relationship between individuals and the state. Now citizens are not only subjects, they are parties to agreements. The state is at the same time controlling authority and an agreement partner. What does this mean in the application or, rather, the absence of application of the rules of the public administration; rules set up in order to prevent abuse of power and to ensure the respect for the legal rights of individuals. Surely the courts of law exercise legal control, but this control foremost focuses on the material content of an agreement, not on controlling the exercise of power. As ombudsmen we must be aware of this trend and realize that this may effect the scope of our control function that is still focused on the government in its traditional role and not in its role as a private subject. In my opinion there is good reason to watch how this development will influence the possibilities of democratic control, transparency, accountability, and sanctions.

Decision-making by Information

I also want to point out something that possibly could be an upcoming trend. We have noticed in Sweden a slight tendency for public boards or agencies to sometimes "govern", not by formal decisions concerning the rights of individuals, but through informal statements. In reality these statements are as binding for the individual as a formal decision. The problem is that these kind of "decisions" cannot be appealed to the public administrative courts and these "decisions" are not based on rules in the *Constitution* and the *Administrative Act*, which are set up to guarantee the legal rights of individuals.

The Supreme Administrative Court in Sweden quite recently passed a judgement regarding this question. Briefly, it concerned whether statements in an information paper distributed by a national board, the National Food Administration, should be regarded as simply and solely information or as an administrative decision comprising a prohibition of the sale of certain olive oil products. After a long discussion the Court found that the contents of the statements were such that the statements should be regarded as an administrative decision. The next question was whether this decision could be appealed against or not. The Court found that, although the statements of the board could not be regarded as formally binding for the company concerned, the statements could not be understood by the company in any other way than binding, in order to make the company withdraw the products from the market. As a consequence, the Court allowed an appeal, not regarding the material content of the statements, but only regarding the question whether the board had exceeded its competence or not. The Court concluded that the board had exceeded its competence in that sense that the board, not clearly separating its task of information from its task of supervision, had gone beyond the limit of what should be comprised in the former task. So, the so-called decision of the National Food Administration was set aside.

Modern Technology: Not Only Advantages?

The development of information technology has an enormous impact on our daily work and will do so in the future. It is certainly a challenge to respond to all the possibilities that it gives us. We have to face the fact, however, that the fast development of technology within public administration has also caused some new problems regarding the relationship between advanced technology and the principle of good public governance. There seems to be a tendency towards giving technology the highest priority and in doing so the application of the legislative rules concerning the administrative procedure is neglected. These rules are of greatest importance as they provide for the legal interests of citizens. Let me give you a very concrete and simple example. Sometimes a decision made by an authority is not understandable, even in the case concerned, because the drafter has used a pre-produced model for writing the decision and has thus forgotten about the individual differences that might be there. So the decision could be absolutely "up in the blue". If you, as ombudsman, receive a complaint about this odd decision and ask the authority for an explanation, the answer could be: the drafter must have pressed the button for the model that seemed to be as close to the case as possible.

Efficiency is often good but surely it should not be allowed to be in opposition to the rights of the individual. As a matter of fact, efficiency is one of the components of these rights. So, in one way or another, we have to deal with the tendency to put traditional values, aimed at upholding high quality within public administration, aside in the interest of mere speediness, outcome measures, and so on. Is computer language and data linguistics, from the citizen's point of view, strengthening or weakening democracy?

Although the principle of good public governance in itself is not put into question, there are—and I can see it in my own daily work—such tendencies within the public administration. It seems as urgent as ever, or even more so, to stress the importance of the principle so it will not be neglected when exercising public power.

50

Consequences of Internationalization and Globalization

Internationalization leads to many advantages, but it also leads to challenges in adapting to new legal systems. The legal environment in which we, as ombudsmen, are acting is extended, at least in Europe, and we must be on our guard in order not to be overrun by this development. We must also keep an eye on the public authorities so that they are aware of the enlargement of the legal framework to which they must adhere. This is constructive work and a true positive challenge.

Unfortunately, internationalization and globalization are also related to problems. Fraud and corruption within public administration are not just crimes. These phenomena are threats to democracy itself. There is a risk that these cancers of many countries in the world are disseminated into other countries, so far mainly spared from the illness. An open administration with transparent procedures has proved to be the best protection against these problems. The challenge for ombudsmen in many countries is to monitor a development towards a public society free from fraud and corruption. The changing need for ombudsmen in countries lucky enough not to suffer seriously from this illness might be to claim the importance of preserving a clean borderline and stress the principle of transparency in public government in order to eliminate the risk of infection.

On the global level we also have to carefully watch what is going on from a legal point of view regarding the struggle against undemocratic influences and terrorist actions. I will just mention it here as an example of what we have to consider in meeting today's changing needs.

I will also briefly mention something that is somewhat related to what I have already said about the shifting in the role of the public government. I think that we, from our ombudsman point of view, must be aware of the risk that internationalization or globalization may gradually change the borderline between what is public service related to good governance under the rule of law and service performed by multinational powers guided by profit, so often ignoring openness and accountability. There is hardly any point in stressing democracy and human rights if the states lose control. This is, of course, foremost a political issue, but we have to fulfil our task as watchdogs in order to prevent a loss of the recognition of all the fundamental principles that every democracy with a well functioning good administration has achieved.

Conclusion

The ombudsmen and, not least, their mandators, the parliaments, must show their will and ability to respond to changes if we want the ombudsman institutions to survive. On a very practical level the ombudsmen must, from time to time, obtain sufficient resources to be able to fulfil the supervisory task and an ombudsman institution must of course adapt to the current circumstances. But as

I have already mentioned, the adaption may not go too far; there are limits. We must always consider, in meeting today's changing needs, the fundamental values that we are entrusted to support. We must not forget that human rights are not taken for granted everywhere. It is a challenge for some countries to work for the recognition of these rights as they are a cornerstone in the concept of democracy. In other countries there must be an ongoing fight to keep and secure these rights. In both cases it is a task for ombudsmen to enhance respect for human dignity by opposing abuse, injustice, and violation of law.

HOW DO YOU KNOW YOU ARE DOING A GOOD JOB?: STRATEGIC PLANS, PERFORMANCE MEASURES, AND SURVEYS

Howard Kushner*

Écrit du point de vue d'un ombudsman, cet article propose de répondre à la question suivante: «Comment savoir si votre bureau fait du bon travail?» Pour ce faire, l'auteur indique qu'il faut d'abord définir la notion de «bon travail», puis déterminer comment appliquer cette notion à l'évaluation de votre bureau. Pour illustrer ce processus, l'auteur, qui est Ombudsman de la province de Colombie-britannique (Canada), discute de la valeur d'un plan d'ensemble et de ses composantes (vision, objectifs et stratégies) pour un bureau d'ombudsman. Il identifie également le processus que son propre bureau a suivi pour mettre en place un plan de ce type.

L'auteur discute ensuite le concept et la valeur des sondages et des mesures de performance qui sont censées démontrer si un bureau fait du «bon travail». Il indique plusieurs outils employés par le Bureau des ombudsmans de la Colombie-britannique. Si certaines données sont faciles à mesurer (temps de réponse et respect des dates limites), d'autres le sont moins (qualité des enquêtes, par exemple). L'auteur fait également des commentaires sur la valeur des sondages, sur les plaignant(e)s, les autorités et le public en général. En dernier lieu, cet article analyse les deux indicateurs que l'auteur a choisis pour mesurer la qualité du

* Howard Kushner, Ombudsman, Province of British Columbia, Canada. Paper delivered at the VIIIth. Conference of the International Ombudsman Institute, September 7-10, 2004, Quebec City, Quebec.

travail effectué par son bureau: (1) le nombre de recommmandations rejetées par les autorités, à la suite d'une enquête; et (2) le pourcentage des enquêtes ayant entraîné des changements positifs dans les pratiques, les politiques, les statuts ou les règlements gouvernementaux.

****

Este artículo brinda la perspectiva de un ombudsman sobre cómo contestar la pregunta siguiente: ¿Cómo sabe Vd. que su oficina está haciendo un buen trabajo? A fin de contestar esta pregunta se debe definir un buen trabajo y cómo se puede demostrar que está bien realizado. El autor, el Ombudsman de la Provincia de British Columbia, Canadá, discute el valor de un plan estratégico para una oficina y las partes del mismo (visión, objetivos y estrategias) para determinar lo que constituye 'un buen trabajo'. También proporciona un esbozo del proceso que sigue su oficina a fin de desarrollar un plan estratégico.

A continuación, el artículo analiza el valor y el concepto de medidas de desempeño y de las encuestas para poder demostrar que una oficina está cumpliendo con su trabajo de manera eficaz. Presenta las medidas de desempeño adoptadas por la Oficina del Ombudsman de British Columbia. Algunos aspectos son más fáciles de evaluar, como por ejemplo si las acciones se realizaron de manera oportuna y la rapidez en responder; otros son más difíciles, tales como la calidad de las investigaciones. El autor también comenta sobre el valor de las encuestas, los demandantes, las autoridades y el público en general. El artículo concluye con una discusión de dos indicadores elegidos por el autor para evaluar la calidad del trabajo en su oficina: (1) el número de investigaciones en las cuales la autoridad se negó a aceptar las recomendaciones (objetivo: que sea cero) y (2) el porcentaje de investigaciones de quejas que condujeron a un cambio positivo en la práctica, políticas, estatutos o reglamentaciones de las autoridades.

Introduction

Shortly after I was appointed Ombudsman for British Columbia in 1999, I was asked, at a meeting, "How do you know that your office is doing a good job"? I thought about it for a minute or two and then began to talk anecdotally about how this case was resolved and that case was settled and how hard my staff was working and how dedicated they are and the positive outcomes we have achieved and the letters of thanks we have received and the changes to procedures and policies that have occurred as a result of our investigations. But after the meeting, I thought about the question some more and realized that before you can answer the question,

"How do you know that your office is doing a good job," you have to know "what a good job" is for your office and how to measure it.

How do you decide what is a "good job?" From whose perspective do you consider—yours, your staff who receive and investigate the complaints, the complainant who comes to your office alleging an unfairness, the authority whose actions or decisions are being called into question, the legislature who created the office, the public who fund the office through their taxes, or the media (TV, radio, and the press) who report on our offices?

This same question can be asked in a slightly different format. In the current economic climate of reduced resources and increased demand for accountability, the buzzwords of "efficiency and effectiveness" are heard over and over again. Two questions are repeatedly asked:

1. Is your office efficient (doing things right)—generally in the context of being timely and cost conscious?

2. Is your office effective (doing the right things)—achieving its goals such as fairness, accountability, and openness in public administration?

I have no magic answers or solutions to these questions, but let me lead you on one ombudsman's journey in search of those elusive answers; to assist in better defining what a "good job" is and how we can demonstrate we are achieving that result.

Let me start the journey with a disclaimer. I am not a management consultant or an organizational restructuring guru. I will not attempt to give you definitions and detailed descriptions. Instead I will tell you what we did in British Columbia from a layman's perspective.

The Strategic Plan

When I was appointed Ombudsman in 1999, our office already had a Strategic Plan for 1997– 2001.[1] It contained the standard stuff—vision, goals, and strategies. As the new Ombudsman, it was important to review the document and to see if I agreed with it and whether any changes were required. For me the most important part of the Strategic Plan is the vision. This, in short, is the "good job" we are trying to do. Through a process of staff consultation and consensus, we revised our Strategic Plan 2001–2005.[2] The vision was restated as "Fairness and Accountability in Public Administration in British Columbia." We also have a short version, "Fairness for BC." The rest of the Strategic Plan, including the *goals*, the *core strategies*, and the *actions*, is the "How"; the vision is the "Job."

In developing a revised Strategic Plan, our office engaged in a process involving all of our staff. This included large staff meetings for all staff and small meetings of groups of staff based upon the existing team and administrative structure. Consultation, in my view, is very important in order to get the input of the staff, including what they see as the role of the office. It also allows you to express your view, on a personal level to the staff, of how you see the role of the office.

Once you have the *vision* then the next steps are how to achieve it—the development of *goals*, the *strategies*, and the *actions* to achieve these goals. The *goals* we set for our office were thorough and impartial investigations, high quality service, high morale in the workplace, and education and public awareness. We then developed *strategies* to achieve each of the goals, focusing on improving the quality of service and quality of investigations, managing workload, and broadening the public profile.

We are now just beginning the process to revisit and revise our 2001-2005 Strategic Plan. I expect the *vision* will remain similar, if not the same, but our *goals* and certainly our *strategies* will change to recognize the different realities of 2004 (smaller office, thirty-five percent budget cut, reduced resources, and telecommuting staff) from the situation in 2001.

If you visit the website of various ombudsman offices or read their annual reports you will see a variety of vision or mission statements: some long, some short, but all with a similar message—fairness and accountability, or promoting high standards of administrative practice and decision making. That's the "good job" we aspire to do.

The more difficult question is "How you know you are doing it?"

How To Measure Performance (Surveys and Performance Measures)

Performance Measures

Having set out what your *vision* is—the next question is how do you determine if you are achieving your *vision*. As is often the case, there are few, if any direct instruments to measure whether you have achieved your vision—in our instance, for example, "Fairness for BC". Instead, we looked at our goals and strategies and asked if we had achieved these. Thus we have to rely on "indirect measures"—in fact, what I would call "twice-removed" indirect measures. In the Strategic Plan we have a *vision*, then *goals* to achieve the *vision*, then *strategies* to achieve the *goals*. Our measurements generally focus on whether we are achieving our strategies, not measuring whether we are achieving our goals, let alone our vision.

So for example—one *goal* in our strategic plan was high quality service and another was thorough investigations. We focused on our investigative approach and strategies—but also on timely and efficient services. I believe it is important for an office to be timely and responsive in its investigation.

Before I explain what we did to meet these goals, let me digress. After I was first appointed, I met with the investigative team leaders and asked, "How long does it take to do an investigation?" I am sure it surprises no one, that the answer I received was, "It depends. Every investigation is different—different facts, different authorities". To me this was not a satisfactory answer. So I rephrased the question: "Are most investigations closed within five years, two years, one year?" The investigative team leaders agreed that most investigations are closed within one year. So we now had at least an end point in mind. After further discussion and after meeting with the investigators and having team leaders meet with their teams—we came up with a set of time frames for investigations.

- seventy percent of files closed within ninety days;
- eighty-five percent of files closed within one hundred and eighty days;
- ninety percent of files closed within one year;
- ninety-five percent of files closed within two years; and
- one hundred percent of files closed within three years.

At that time, we also had a backlog of older files. We set targets for how many of our files would be older than one year:

- in 2002 less than twenty percent;
- in 2003 less than fifteen percent; and
- in 2004 less than ten percent.

We also set standards of performance for contacting complainants:

- within five working days of the file being assigned to an investigator; and

- contact with a complainant at least once every ninety days to inform them of the status of the investigation.

To insure that files are reviewed in a timely manner in order to decide whether to investigate, we set standards of:

- making a decision whether to commence an investigation within thirty days of a file being assigned to an investigator, and

- notice to an authority within thirty days of decision to investigate.

As our intake function is separated from our investigative function (we receive about 9,000 to 10,000 complaints and enquiries in a year, approximately 200 per week), we have a specialized intake team. Again, in consultation with the intake team, performance measures were established for their work:

- phone calls returned within four hours; and

- responses to letters, faxes, and internet-filed complaints—within two working days.

These measures assist in responding to the question, "Are we being efficient?" They assist in answering the question "are you doing a good job" by showing how we deal with the process of the investigation—our timeliness and responsiveness. They do not directly address the issue of the quality of the work done.

We also have as a *goal*—education and public awareness and a strategy of increasing the public profile and awareness of the office. Again, we engaged in a variety of activities to assist in achieving this goal, for example—posting all our public reports on our website, and doing provincial tours or public outreach to various areas of the province to increase public awareness.

I believe that it is important to issue special public reports in addition to the annual report. These special reports need not be about one specific investigation but rather instead may address issues of general significance relating to administrative fairness. For example, our office, over the past five years, has issued three special reports which were not case specific but rather addressed general issues of fairness. In September 2001, we issued Public Report No. 40 entitled *"Developing an Internal Complaint Mechanism"*[3] which was written to assist public authorities in developing their own internal processes to review complaints. A number of authorities have referred to this report when reviewing existing internal complaint procedures or in developing new ones. In March 2003, we issued Public Report No. 42, *"Code of Administrative Justice 2003"*.[4] This code set out standards for administrative fairness which we apply to decide whether an authority's decision, recommendation, or act was fair. Both reports also operated as an educational tool to inform the public about the practices of the office. We also issued Special Report No. 24, *"Acting in the Public Interest? Self-Governance in the Health Professions: The Ombudsman's Perspective"* in May 2003.[5] This report provided comments on the ten years that our office has investigated complaints about the self-governing bodies that regulate professionals in health disciplines. The report highlighted the importance and need for public accountability in the self-governing health professions. These three reports contribute to our vision of "Fairness for BC" by providing general comments about administrative fairness, serving an educational need, and promoting changes where needed, or supporting existing programs and policies where appropriate.

In addition to our own internal measures, we also decided to conduct four surveys. One survey addressed public awareness, two addressed service to complainants and authorities respectively, and the fourth addressed staff job satisfaction.

We conducted a general public survey—asking questions about knowledge of our office. A high percentage of people had heard of the "Office of the Ombudsman"—seventy-three percent, but only nineteen percent knew what we did—what you might call high name recognition but low product recognition. So, in response, we are developing a more focused public awareness campaign including three five-minute videos about the office. These videos will be shown on the "Knowledge Network", a public education TV network available throughout BC. Also, the videos will be "streamed" off our website,[6] so that anyone can view them. In addition, teaching materials have been developed for two grade levels in high school, Social Studies Eleven and Law Twelve, to encourage the use of the videos in school curriculums.

We also surveyed complainants and authorities with respect to their experience with us. "Were they treated with respect and courtesy?", "Were we accessible?", "Was the process explained to them?" For the most part, on these types of questions, we scored well. But on the question of whether the complainant was satisfied with the process, we scored lowered than I expected. Only forty-eight percent of the complainants surveyed were satisfied with the process of the investigation. We also discovered that there was a high correlation between the outcome of the investigation and satisfaction with the process. Ninety-one percent, of those who agreed with the outcome of the investigation were satisfied with the process whereas only twenty-six percent of those who disagreed with the outcome were satisfied with the process. This was repeated in the authority survey—more were satisfied with the process—eighty-eight percent, but the correlation factor was ninety-four percent of authorities who agreed with the outcome were satisfied while only six percent who disagreed were satisfied with the process.

These sets of figures are important pieces of the puzzle involving the issues "Are we being effective?", and "Are we doing a good job from the complainant and authorities perspective?" We intend to continue to do these types of surveys either on an ongoing basis or on a periodic basis.

How to Measure Quality

But even with all this information—timely performance, responses of complainants and authorities, educating the public—have we answered the question, "Are you doing a good job?". I believe we have answered it in part. We have responded to some of the efficiency/effectiveness issues; we have identified how we measure doing a good job. But to me, at least, I was still not satisfied that we had answered the *quality question*, "Are we doing a *good* job?" as opposed to, "Are we doing our job good?".

After discussion with senior staff, I decided to choose two indicators to try to reflect on the quality of our work and, to report on those in my annual report. These indicators are a more direct response to whether we were bringing "Fairness to BC". The two indicators chosen were:

1. The number of investigations where the authority refused to accept our recommendation (target goal: zero); and

2. The percentage of complaint investigations that lead to a positive change in practice, policies, statutes, or regulations by authorities.

If our vision is "Fairness for BC", one way to measure that is the extent to which authorities are responsive to our office and are prepared to amend or change their decisions and actions to respond to our "fairness" concerns. Further, the second indicator, the change in policy and practice reflects systemic change which hopefully results in "fairness" improvements for many, not just for one. In 2002, nineteen percent of our closed investigation files had an impact beyond the individual who made the complaint and resulted in positive change in practice, policies, statutes, or regulation. In 2003, the percentage was smaller at eight percent.

One comment I have received about the two factors I have chosen is that both are determined not by what any office does but instead by the actions of the authorities in responding to us. That is—we are measuring our performance by whether we are having an impact on the administrative process, not simply in identifying "unfairness" but in having the unfairness remedied and removed. Some may argue that our success should be determined by our work, not by how others respond to our work. But if part of doing a "good job" is improving the administrative process, then measuring change may be an important way of demonstrating that.

Conclusion

It would be remiss of me to suggest that our office has all the answers. We do not and we know it. Much work has been done on strategic planning, performance measures, and surveys by many other offices. Certainly the work of the various Australian ombudsman offices, the New Zealand Office of Ombudsmen as well as the Parliamentary Commissioner for Administration in the United Kingdom should be acknowledged. Their experiences have provided much assistance to our office in pursuit of the "Holy Grail".

Also, we should not ignore the positive outcomes and results achieved in the individual investigations carried out by our staff. Every year, in my annual report, I provide case examples of complaints investigated and resolved through the actions of our office. These are our individual quality assurance mechanisms. The difficulty is in translating these anecdotal individual cases to a measure of "quality" performance.

It is also important to recognize that the successes of the office are the result of the hard work of the staff. There is no doubt that within our office, there has been a substantial change in the work environment due in part to budget cuts (closure of an office, creation of telecommuting opportunities) and in part to changes in procedure (establishment of formal performance measures, biannual case status reviews). Yet, throughout this process, our staff have remained focused on their work and on providing high quality service. The quality of the work done by our office is a direct reflection of the quality of the staff who performed it.

In conclusion, let me again state that this paper is one ombudsman's journey. It speaks to how we, my staff and I, attempted to find answers to what at first glance appears to be a simple question. It is not a template for all offices to follow. Its value, if any, is in the telling, in the experience of trying to find the answer to the question. I would be very interested in hearing of your experience in responding to the question, in developing your own "quality" performance measure, in determining your "vision" for your offices. All of us have, in some form or other, faced the same question; all of us have developed answers for the question.

Endnotes

1.   Office of the Ombudsman of British Columbia, *Ombuds Strategic Plan 1997-2001*, Special Report No. 20 (British Columbia: Office of the Ombudsman of British Columbia, 1998), online: Office of the Ombudsman of British Columbia <http://www.ombudsman.bc.ca/reports/strategic_plan/1997-2001/index.htm>.

2.   Office of the Ombudsman of British Columbia, *The 2001-2005 B.C. Ombudsman Strategic Plan*, Special Report No. 22 (British Columbia: Office of the Ombudsman of British Columbia, 2001), online: Office of the Ombudsman of British Columbia <http://www.ombudsman.bc.ca/reports/strategic_plan/2001-2005/StrategicPlan_2001-2005.pdf>.

3.   Office of the Ombudsman of British Columbia, *Developing an Internal Complaint Mechanism*, Public Report No. 40 (British Columbia: Office of the Ombudsman of British Columbia, 2001), online: Office of the Ombudsman of British Columbia

<http://www.ombudsman.bc.ca/reports/Public
_Reports/PR40_ICM/PR40_ICM.pdf>.

4.   Office of the Ombudsman of British Columbia, *Code of Administrative
        Justice 2003*, Public Report No. 42 (British Columbia: Office of the
        Ombudsman of British Columbia, 2003), online: Office of the
        Ombudsman of British Columbia
        <http://www.ombudsman.bc.ca/reports/Public_Reports/Public%20Repo
        rt%2042.pdf>.

5.   Office of the Ombudsman of British Columbia, *Acting in the Public
        Interest? Self-Governance in the Health Professions: The Ombudsman's
        Perspective*, Special Report No. 24 (British Columbia: Office of the
        Ombudsman of British Columbia, 2003), online: Office of the
        Ombudsman of British Columbia
        <http://www.ombudsman.bc.ca/reports/Public_Reports/Special%20Re/
        ort%20 No. 2042.pdf>.

6.   See online: Office of the Ombudsman of British Columbia
        <http://www.ombudsman.bc.ca>.

Bibliography

Office of the Ombudsman of British Columbia. *2002 Annual Report*
(British Columbia: Office of the Ombudsman of British Columbia, 2002),
online: Office of the Ombudsman of British Columbia
<http://www.ombudsman.bc.ca/publication/index.htm>.

Office of the Ombudsman of British Columbia. *2003 Annual Report*
(British Columbia: Office of the Ombudsman of British Columbia, 2003),
online: Office of the Ombudsman of British Columbia
<http://www.ombudsman.bc.ca/publication/index.htm>.

Office of the Ombudsman of British Columbia. *Ombuds Strategic Plan
1997-2001*, Special Report No. 20 (British Columbia: Office of the
Ombudsman of British Columbia, 1998), online: Office of the
Ombudsman of British Columbia
<http://www.ombudsman.bc.ca/reports/strategic_plan/1997-
2001/index.htm>.

Office of the Ombudsman of British Columbia. *The 2001 - 2005
B.C. Ombudsman Strategic Plan*, Special Report No. 22 (British
Columbia: Office of the Ombudsman of British Columbia, 2001), online:
Office of the Ombudsman of British
Columbia<http://www.ombudsman.bc.ca/reports
/strategic_plan/2001-2005/StrategicPlan_2001-2005.pdf>.

Office of the Ombudsman of British Columbia. *Service Plan
2004/05*-2006/07 (British Columbia: Office of the Ombudsman of
British Columbia, 2004), online: Office of the Ombudsman of British
Columbia
<http://www.ombudsman.bc.ca/reports/Report_2004/Service%20Plan%
202004%20%202007.pdf>.

SPECIAL PROTECTION REQUIREMENTS FOR MINORITIES: THE PARLIAMENTARY COMMISSIONER FOR THE RIGHTS OF NATIONAL AND ETHNIC MINORITIES OF HUNGARY

Jenő Kaltenbach*

Dans cet article, l'auteur étudie la mise en place de la législation européenne et des institutions juridiques dans le domaine de la protection des droits des minorités. Prenant l'exemple de la Hongrie, il analyse les responsabilités du Commissaire parlementaire aux droits nationaux et à ceux des minorités ethniques, et il évalue son efficacité dans ce domaine. L'auteur conclut que le meilleur moyen de s'acquitter de ses fonctions d'ombudsman n'est pas de prendre le rôle de protecteur des minorités, mais d'être un juge impartial des droits de ces minorités.

****

El autor analiza el desarrollo de la ley europea y de las instituciones legales en cuanto a la protección de las minorías. Explora las funciones principales del Comisionado Parlamentario para los Derechos de las Minorías Nacionales y Étnicas de Hungría, y también evalúa su efectividad en la protección de los derechos de tales grupos. El autor concluye que en vez de actuar como un

* Parliamentary Commissioner for the Rights of National and Ethnic Minorities of Hungary. Paper delivered at the European Ombudsman Institute Conference, May 10, 2004 and at the International Ombudsman Institute VIIIth International Ombudsman Conference, Québec City, Canada, September 7-10, 2004.

protector de minorías, la función más efectiva del ombudsman es de ser un juez
neutral de los derechos de las mismas.

The Rights of Minorities and the Ombudsman

Hardly any other public institution has more to do with the idea that the weak are in need of protection against the strong and powerful than the ombudsman. There are hardly any bigger differences between positions of power than the difference found between that of a citizen belonging to a minority community and the almighty bureaucracy of the nation state. This should lead to a logical conclusion that the key function of an ombudsman—the protection of the rights of citizens—is most completely developed in this very relationship, but this is not true. The reason for this is very simple: an ombudsman may protect only what is guaranteed by the legal system, but no ombudsman may protect something that does not exist. The rights of minorities were, for quite some time, not included in the list of internationally recognized human rights. This situation has changed materially only during the past decade, but the emancipation of the rights of minorities cannot be considered as fully resolved, even today. A paradigm change is, nevertheless, underway both in terms of the international law and the national legislation of numerous European nation states. The changes I am talking about are evident in two aspects. On the one hand, concrete actions are taken in order to protect minorities' rights. On the other hand, the system of the legal institutions against ethnic (racial) discrimination is developing steadily. The work under the frameworks of the Council of Europe and the European Union are of particular importance for us.

From among the numerous documents on this topic prepared by the Council of Europe, special mention should be made of the European Charter of Regional or Minority Languages,[1] the Framework Convention for the Protection of National Minorities[2] and Protocol No. 12 to the Convention on the Protection of Human Rights and Fundamental Freedoms, on the general prohibition of negative discrimination.[3] Mention should also be made of the European Commission against Racism and Intolerance (ECRI), which has elaborated the principles and institutions of combating ethnic discrimination in a number of General Policy Recommendations. The most important relevant document of the European Union is Council Directive 2000/43/EC on the implementation of equal treatment of people regardless of race and ethnic origins.[4]

At the same time, a number of European countries have adopted specific acts on the protection of minorities, introduced such provisions in their bodies of law, and adopted anti-discriminatory laws during recent years.

As a matter of course, the effectiveness of such normative changes does not primarily hinge on the institutional background set up in order to actually enforce the legal regulations. This concept is also encountered in the above noted European documents as well—particularly in EU Directive No. 2000/43—but ECRI's General Policy Recommendation No. 2 deals with the parameters of such a specialized body in even more detail, laying out the following requirements with respect to such a body:

a.   it should aim at ensuring the elimination of the various forms of discrimination, the promotion of equal opportunities, and the development of good relations between people belonging to different groups of society;

b.   it should monitor the contents and scopes of legislation and the implementing decrees with a view to their implications concerning racism, xenophobia, anti-Semitism, and intolerance and should make proposals concerning amendments to legislation where necessary;

c.   by providing advice, it should assist the authorities in charge of legislation and execution, with respect to the improvement of the regulations and practices relating to the areas in question;

d.   it should provide assistance and support to victims—including legal aid—to ensure the enforcement and exercise of their rights before institutions and courts;

e.   there should be legal remedies available subject to the legal framework of the given country (before courts and other judicial authorities)—as required;

f.   it should receive and consider complaints and applications with respect to specific cases and make efforts to promote the resolution of problems through negotiations or—within limits specified by law—through binding and enforceable decisions;

g. it should have proper powers for the collection of the evidence and information required for the performance of its tasks laid out in the above item;

h. it should provide information and advice for the bodies and institutions concerned—including the relevant public bodies and institutions;

i. it should provide advice in respect of the norms required for the elimination of discrimination in specific areas, which may then become either norms prescribed by law on a mandatory basis or norms to be applied on a voluntary basis;

j. it should support and, by its active participation, help the training of the various main groups—without prejudice to the primary training roles of the relevant trade organizations;

k. it should promote awareness raising in society concerning the main questions of discrimination and should produce and publish adequate information and documents;

l. it should support and encourage the operations of organizations aiming at goals similar to those of the specialized body; and

m. it should take into account and communicate, if necessary, the concerns of such organizations and issues they consider important.

According to the recommendation, depending on the legal traditions of the country concerned, such an organ may be: a national committee for racial equality, an ombudsman against ethnic discrimination, a centre/office combating racism and fighting for equality of opportunities, or other appropriate forms, including bodies working on realizing goals pertaining to the wider field of general human rights. The special ombudsman approach is also supported by the Eide report produced for the United Nations.[5] Several of the member states of the Council of Europe have set up institutions specializing in the fight against racial/ethnic discrimination,[6] but the special ombudsman arrangement has so far only been adopted by Sweden, Finland, and Hungary.[7]

The Parliamentary Commissioner for the Rights of National and Ethnic Minorities of Hungary

The Hungarian institution of the Parliamentary Commissioner for the Rights of National and Ethnic Minorities is a parliamentary ombudsman institution, independent both from the executive and the judicial power. The Commissioner is appointed by the Parliament of the Republic of Hungary and he reports to Parliament. His independence of the executive power is indubitable along each of the three factors specified in the ECRI's General Policy Recommendation No. 2: he is independent in terms of the budget; he performs his tasks without state intervention, *i.e.* he enjoys autonomy in terms of the appointment of his employees, management of his resources, and in forming his opinion; and, finally, he has personal autonomy, because the *Act on the Parliamentary Commissioner* contains guarantees with respect to the appointment and withdrawal of the Ombudsman.

The Ombudsman institution assumes an important role in the formulation of anti-discriminatory objectives in Hungary. The Parliamentary Commissioner for Minorities actively participates in the assessment of the implementation of the anti-discriminatory measures as well as in the continued development and transformation of the legal framework. All of the official assessments, audits, and investigations of the Ombudsman are completed by the institution's formulation of various recommendations for the various ministries concerned with proposals addressing the modernization of the legal framework. Most of the recommendations concerning the continued development of the legal framework have been formulated in relation to the investigation of concrete complaints.

Finally, the Parliamentary Commissioner for Minorities participates in the legislation process and the political decision making processes. His opinion is sought in relation to each new act or amendment that has an influence on his institution or in respect of all issues with which his institution has to deal including, amongst other things, the anti-discriminatory regulations and legislation. Indeed, the fact that the Ombudsman for Minorities made a proposal concerning the draft of the anti-discrimination legislation in year 2000 to the Ministry of Justice and to the Parliament's Committee for Human Rights, Minorities and Religious Affairs, is an indication of his interpretation of the autonomy of the institution and its participation in the performance of the tasks of the executive power in an even broader sense: he considers the submission of proposals concerning legislative changes as part of his tasks, but he will also participate in the work of the legislative power.

Scope of Tasks

The traditional model of the ombudsman permits only investigations pertaining to the operations of the public administration system.

Unfortunately, the Hungarian legal environment defines the functioning of the institution of the Hungarian Parliamentary Commissioner for Minorities on the basis of the traditional model of the ombudsman institution. This recognized conflict can be resolved by indirect action. The state is in charge of permitting (licensing) private enterprises, enforcing contracts, and exercising legality supervision over a number of operations, most of which are in fact activities of private actors proceeding in the public sector. Indirectly, the control exercised by the Ombudsman may be extended to violations of human rights that are committed in various areas of the private sector.

One of the large areas of the manifestation of racial discrimination is private enterprise, *i.e.* the business sector. By their employment policies, appointment principles, and the selection of customers, private enterprises may discriminate against members of disadvantaged ethnic groups. Certain indirect measures may take place in the area of services offered by private enterprises and the employment of private market actors.

The Functions of the Institution

According to the opinion considered as dominant in technical literature with respect to the institution of the Ombudsman for Minorities, three main groups of functions and obligations may be identified in relation to the operations of such institutions:

- political decision making and legislative functions,
- functions of law enforcement (enabling the exercise of rights), and
- information and education/awareness raising functions.

According to the above three groups of functions, the institution of the Ombudsman for Minorities may address the problem of racial discrimination at each of the three levels where this problem may arise. In the exercise of its rights concerning the information of the public and education/awareness raising, the institution acts against racist declarations, racial prejudice, and racial discrimination at the level of the values jointly assumed by the members of society. Its executive rights and its rights concerning the review of policies and legislation as well as the right to make proposals concerning the development of policies and legislation operate at the other two levels. From the aspect of the second level—action against the application of discriminatory methods—the institution's executive powers are of particular importance, including executive rights pertaining to concrete complaints along with its strategic rights. The third level—the spreading of ideas and methods aiming at giving rise to racial hatred— may be addressed primarily by the rights of the institution concerning the publication of guidelines on good methods, codes of behaviour, and recommendations for the participants of society including employees, local governments, health institutions, insurance companies, and the state. Let us review these three groups of functions and competences one by one.

a) Legislative and Political Decision Making Functions

I have already touched upon the legislative and political decision making functions of the institution relating to its autonomy. It is clear from the above that as an Ombudsman for Minorities I take a broad interpretation of the legislative and political decision making functions provided for by law. We review relevant laws and other legal regulations on a regular basis. This comprehensive analysis is concluded by the elaboration of recommendations concerning amendments to the laws in effect, along with the drafting of proposals concerning new laws and amendments. In the analysis of concrete complaints, the recommendations are sometimes focused on the modification only of local decrees, but even in such cases we often turn to the ministries and make recommendations concerning the review of national level legal regulations, particularly in cases where problems occur repeatedly or in cases raising institutional problems of discrimination.

A certain practice has evolved during the past years in the preparation of drafts of new acts of law. Ministries ask for comments by the Ombudsman during the process of the preparation of laws.

b) Executive Functions

Another set of functions available for the Parliamentary Commissioner for Minorities is comprised of the execution of the anti-discrimination regulations. As for the various concrete cases, complaints may be submitted by victims, any non-governmental organs, or any other organization. The office launched investigations in many cases on the basis of news published by the media. The procedure of submitting complaints is highly informal: the complainant submits his/her complaint in writing or, on the basis of a complaint by word of mouth, an employee of the office drafts the request. The office may also be contacted by telephone to make complaints. Based on documents supplied by the institution against which a complaint has been submitted, the Ombudsman carries out the investigation or visits the site and talks to eye witnesses and others involved in the case. Such features of the institution enable the investigation of separate cases of discrimination that would have remained unexplored without such an institution.

One major advantage of the institution is the possibility of onsite investigations which enables a thorough analysis of cases and the collection of the largest amount of information on the issues at hand. Investigations carried out at the locations of affairs of discrimination have always proven to be highly useful.

As for the exercise of the executive powers, the other dominant feature of the institution is the use of instruments available for the investigation of cases of discrimination, such as:

- intermediation,
- reconciliation,
- convincing, and
- publicity.

In the case of some of the complaints submitted to the office we find that no rights have been abused, no racial discrimination has taken place, and the cause of the complaint is primarily the lack of information and the lack of adequate communication between the authorities and complainants, which is often experienced by the complainant as discrimination. In other cases, the complaint is fully justified and well-founded, but the Ombudsman has no competence to initiate an investigation. In such cases, the office either intermediates between the parties, facilitating better flows of information, informs the complainant of other possibilities and means of legal remedy available for the complainant or, if necessary, the office forwards the complaint—together with justifications—to the competent institution.

Reconciliation is a method in line with the characteristics of offices similar to the Ombudsman for Minorities and our office makes efforts to apply this technique.

Convincing those concerned is another non-contradictory means available for the Parliamentary Commissioner to settle of cases of discrimination. Convincing means that the Ombudsman relies on the prestige of the institution and his or her personality to convince the person that has committed the discrimination about the detrimental nature of the activity constituting the subject of the complaint, by arguments and explanations.

In the area of strategic powers the Ombudsman also has complete competency. In certain concrete cases he initiates investigations *ex officio* so there is no need for the victim to make a complaint. In order to promote the implementation of strategic goals, a number of general types of official investigations have also been carried out. The education of minorities has been review *inter alia*, a separate investigation was initiated to explore the reasons for the disproportionately high ratios of Roma children in special schools. In the framework of the investigation, attention was paid to the minority local governmental system and the election of the members of minority self governments, and the discrimination experienced in the area of housing and employment. These investigations initiated by the Ombudsman appear to have sufficiently replaced class action[8] which is an institution not included in the Hungarian legal system.

c) Information and Education Functions

Finally, let me describe the third group of the functions of the institution of the Ombudsman for Minorities: these are information and education functions. The powers concerning information include, in accordance with the ECRI recommendation, the provision of information and consultancy support for the bodies and institutions concerned. The provision of consultancy assistance for the participants of the various concrete areas concerns:

- the norms of anti-discriminatory practices,

- participation in the training of the various important groups of society in relation to tolerance and anti-racism and anti-discriminatory methods,

- the communication of issues of discrimination to society including the compiling and dissemination of information and other documents, and, finally

- cooperation with organizations working for the same objectives as the relevant specialized institution.

The Office of the Hungarian Minority Ombudsman has so far published a manual in order to promote cooperation between minority self-governments and local governments concerning the legal frameworks of their operations, including descriptions of concrete relevant cases. Two international conferences have been organized by the Office, one on the representation of minorities and their participation in the political decision making processes, and another one on racial discrimination. The lessons drawn from the conferences have been published in two volumes. The Ombudsman delivers presentations on a regular basis and he contributes to conferences, consultations, and discussions across the country. We have participated in the preparation and implementation of various specialized training courses for, *inter alia,* members of minority self-governments, mayors, and local civil servants.

The institution carries out its educatory and extension training function in an indirect way even when it develops recommendations for various authorities, applies the method of convincing as a means of problem solving, and prepares and submits the annual reports to Parliament.

In my opinion, the institution cannot in any way be considered to be a civil rights actor or a protector of minority rights: the institution is to act in relation to minority rights as a neutral judge. The interpretation of this concept, however, is a delicate issue. Some experts would support the institution of a less "traditional" ombudsman, one that would be more like a non-governmental organization for human rights. In this case, however, we would have to reckon with the loss of the support of a major part of the public which, on the other hand, is the most effective instrument of the Ombudsman.

Conclusion

The Hungarian Minority Ombudsman has been functioning for almost nine years. During this period of time the Ombudsman has taken a variety of actions in response to more than 4,000 complaints. In view of the experience accumulated so far, the following are some of the most important requests for change that have emerged with respect to the mandate of the institution:

> - Directive 2000/43/EC prescribes the setting up of a special "independent authority" in the EU Member States. The *Act on Equal Treatment*[9] was adopted in Hungary accordingly, but the function of an "independent authority" is provided for—instead of extending the mandate of the already functioning Ombudsman for Minorities—through the establishment of a separate parallel public administration organization whose details have not yet been identified. In addition to the fact that this does not meet the requirement of independence, this arrangement entails a threat of the development of unnecessary parallel functions and confusions of competences. The resulting debate has pointed out whether the mandate of the special Ombudsman for Minorities (against discrimination) may be kept within the framework and limits that are characteristic of the traditional parliamentary ombudsman (under public law). In my view, the mandate of the Commissioner for the Protection of Minorities should be extended to the private sector as well, as is recommended by the EU Directive.

> - Another relevant discussion point is whether such an Ombudsman may make binding decisions (e.g. ones establishing the fact of discrimination or imposing fines). According to some, this would not be compatible with the institution of the ombudsman. Others—including myself—are of the opinion that such a "break-up" of the traditional ombudsman model has already taken place in an other area—the protection of personal data—on the basis of the EU Directive on Data Protection.[10] Following this principle in respect of another specialized commissioner would not only not be incompatible, indeed, this would be a logical step and would even be in line both with EU

documents and other relevant documents of the Council of
Europe, already referred to earlier in the paper.

Endnotes

1.   November 5, 1992, Eur. T.S. No. 148 (entered into force March 1, 1998).

2.   February 1, 1995, Eur. T.S. No. 157 (entered into force February 1, 1998).

3.   November 4, 2000, Eur. T.S. No. 177 (entered into force March 1, 2005).

4.   EC, *Council Directive 2000/43 of June 29, 2000 implementing the*
principle of equal treatment between persons irrespective of race or ethnic
origin, [2000] O.J. L. 180/22. The Directive had to be transposed into the
legislation of the Member States by July 19, 2003. This process has not
been concluded as yet.

5.   UN, "Eide-bericht zum Minderheitenschutz, Empfehlungen" in Florin
Ermacora, *Volksgruppenschutz in Europa* (Wien, 1995) 117.

6.   Examples include the Commission for Racial Equality (CRE) in Great
Britain, the Equal Treatment Commission in The Netherlands, or Le
Centre Pour L'egalité Des Chances Et La Lutte Contre Le Racisme in
Belgium. See E.C.R.I, *Exemples de bonnes pratiques: organs spécialisés*
dans la lutte contre le racism, la xénophobie, l'antisémitisme et
l'intolérance au nivea national, CRI (99) 43, April, 1999.

7.   The Hungarian so-called Minorities Ombudsman is the only parliamentary
commissioner in Europe in operation since June 30, 1995. The other two
are so-called governmental ombudsmen.

8.   Class action—a legal procedure initiated by one or more complainants on
his/her or their own behalf and on behalf of all other persons influenced
in a similar way by the given illegal act.

9.   *Act CXXV of 2003 on equal treatment and promotion of equality of*
opportunities (Hungary) entered into force on January 27, 2004. The
specialized authority to be charged with the administration of such issues
will only be set up in early 2005.

10.   EC, *Directive 95/46/EC of the European Parliament and of the Council on the protection of individuals with regard to the processing of personal data and the free movement of such data*, [1995] O.J. L. 281/31). This Directive was adopted on October 24, 1995.

A FIRST NATIONS OMBUDSMAN:
SOME CONSIDERATIONS

Lisa Statt Foy*

Certaines communautés autochtones ressentent un niveau croissant d'insatisfaction, et cette situation a amené les premières nations et le gouvernement fédéral canadien à envisager la création d'un poste d'ombudsman des premières nations. On sait les succès que l'institution de l'ombudsman a remportés dans la promotion des principes de bonne gouvernance, et les gens considèrent cette institution comme une sorte de «caméléon culturel»: la création d'un poste d'ombudsman des premières nations semble donc évidente. Cet article va pourtant à l'encontre de l'attitude qui tend à croire que l'institution de l'ombudsman est culturellement neutre. Rappelant les critères d'efficacité essentiels qu'ont définis les Nations unies et diverses associations d'ombudsmans, l'auteure démontre que ces critères «essentiels» participent de la culture euro-américaine et des valeurs occidentales. Elle analyse à quel point ces caractéristiques essentielles de l'institution de l'ombudsman peuvent différer des valeurs de certaines premières nations, de leurs croyances et de leurs pratiques traditionnelles. L'auteure suggère aux communautés autochtones qui considèrent établir un poste d'ombudsman des premières nations de se livrer, tout d'abord, à un processus d'autoanalyse, d'examiner leurs croyances et leurs pratiques ancestrales, ainsi que les valeurs de la société contemporaine dans laquelle ils vivent. L'auteure conclut que seules les communautés autochtones elles-mêmes, grâce à ce processus d'introspection, sont à même de décider si le

* LL.B., University of Alberta (2004). Currently clerking with the Alberta Court of Appeal and Court of Queen's Bench, and articling with Field Law LLP, Calgary, Alberta, 2005-2006.

modèle de l'ombudsman peut être adapté afin de tenir pleinement compte de leur identité culturelle et répondre aux besoins de leurs membres.

****

La falta de satisfacción en algunas comunidades indígenas canadienses (First Nations) ha causado que dichas comunidades y el gobierno federal canadiense consideraran el establecimiento de un ombudsman propio. La creación de un cargo de ombudsman pareciera ser una solución casi intuitiva, dado su éxito en la promoción de los principios de buena gobernabilidad y la creencia general de que la institución del ombudsman es un camaleón culural. Este artículo desafía la percepción de que la institución del ombudsman es culturalmente neutral. Utilizando los criterios de eficiencia esenciales establecidos por las asociaciones de ombudsmen y los de las Naciones Unidas, la autora explora cómo los criterios 'esenciales' de la institución están basados en valores occidentales y de la cultura euro-americana. Analiza el hecho de que las características esenciales de la institución del ombudsman pueden ser marcadamente divergentes de los valores, creencias y prácticas de algunas comunidades indígenas canadienses. La autora sugiere que las comunidades aborígenes que consideran la posibilidad de establecer una institución de ombudsman se dediquen primero a un proceso de instrospección. Deben revisar las creencias y prácticas tradicionales e identificar los valores contemporáneos. La autora concluye señalando que sólo las comunidades por sí mismas, por medio de este proceso de introspección, pueden determinar si el modelo de ombudsman puede ser adaptado para abarcar su identidad cultural y responder a las necesidades de sus miembros.

"Culture hides much more than it reveals, and strangely enough what it
hides, it hides most effectively from its own participants."
Edward Twitchell Hall, *The Silent Language*[1]

Introduction

Dissatisfaction within some First Nation communities as to the lack of an effective forum for discussing band council and band administration issues, such as alleged electoral inconsistencies, unjust welfare denials, and favouritism in housing and employment allocations, has prompted a search for an appropriate and effective dispute resolution mechanism. Within the federal government, discussions have centred on establishing a parliamentary ombudsman on reserves.[2] Others seeking solutions, such as Chief Roberta Jamieson (Chief of the Six Nations of the Grand River Territory and former Ombudsman for Ontario), have proposed the establishment of a First Nation Ombudsman:[3] an unique ombudsman office that

77

would be responsive and accountable solely to the First Nation community—and independent of the federal government. The latter requirement would make the First Nation Ombudsman markedly different from the "impartial person or body" mandated under s. 11 of *Bill C-7*[4] or the parliamentary ombudsman proposed in two recent private members' bills.[5]

Chief Jamieson, in her paper entitled "The First Nation Ombudsman," details the process by which the ombudsman institution could be translated into the First Nations context.[6] Organizations such as the United Nations,[7] the United States Ombudsman Association,[8] the American Bar Association,[9] and the Ombudsman Association[10] have published essential characteristics, effectiveness criteria, standards, and models for the ombudsman institution. With the assistance of these standards and the benefit of Chief Jamieson's detailed recommendations specific to the aboriginal setting, the ombudsman function could be fairly fluidly transplanted to reserves. However, in my view, introducing the ombudsman institution into First Nation communities—without the respective First Nation first considering the content of their own values, beliefs, and traditional practices and the extent to which the ombudsman institution reinforces or denigrates from their own cultural identity—is unadvisable and potentially detrimental.

This article will explore the essential characteristics of the ombudsman institution, as set out by various ombudsman associations and the United Nations, to illustrate that these qualities are not culturally-neutral but reflect western values and philosophy. Moreover, the analysis will be used to evaluate how the critical elements of the institution may run contrary to a First Nation's values, beliefs, and traditional practices—and, consequently, not be an appropriate dispute resolution instrument for all First Nations communities.

The First Nations Ombudsman

The issues that an aboriginal ombudsman would be established to address can be broadly categorized as concerns relating to "good governance." The essentials of good governance are participation, fairness, and accountability[11]—the latter includes "access to information, transparency in decision-making, and rules of procedural fairness such as the communication of decisions and the reasons on which they are based."[12] Good governance entails "a professional civil service, elimination of corruption in government, a predictable, transparent and accountable administration, democratic decision-making, the supremacy of the rule of law, effective protection of human rights, an independent judiciary, a fair economic system, [and] appropriate devolution and decentralization of government."[13] Generally speaking, the ombudsman institution has enjoyed worldwide success in promoting these tenants of good governance. However, the institution cannot be detached from the political context in which, and for which, it was created: "a national human rights institution will find it extremely difficult to function in a state without a democratic system of checks on the exercise of power, where real independence from the ruling power is not possible and where human rights are not respected in law and/or practice."[14] Governments throughout the world that (to a greater or lesser degree) share such a political orientation have wholesale embraced the ombudsman as an institution of accountability with respect to the public administration. This willingness of government to adopt the institution may lie in the fact that it is carefully crafted to work seamlessly within the system: "[s]ince the Ombudsman may only make recommendations, and may not compel the executive and judicial agencies to take substantive actions, the Ombudsman's role is consistent with the concept of separation of powers."[15] Some would argue that the institution is not only designed to work *within* the system, but also designed to work *for* the system by "neutralizing conflict," thereby ensuring that "the domination of state and capital" are never really directly—or, in fact, indirectly—challenged.[16]

Despite the ombudsman's union with a specific political context, the ombudsman is widely believed to be a cultural chameleon: adaptable to any democratic or democratizing framework. Thus, societies widely divergent from the ombudsman's euro-american motherland, including First Nations, have been inclined to adapt and adopt the institution. However, there is mounting concern about the desirability of responding to First Nations' legal, social, and political needs by simply "indigenizing" western institutions. Michelle LeBaron, in her opening address to the *National Canadian Forum on Intercultural Dispute Resolution*, described how power differentials between aboriginal culture and western culture—which are latently reproduced and reinforced in western institutions—potentially impact aboriginal cultural identity. Where "indigenized" institutions are adopted, western practices can "come to be viewed as "right and necessary," while other ways get labelled as "alternative".[17] This process, which may have fateful results for aboriginal wisdom, is exacerbated by the effect of "internalized oppression": the propensity of "victims of colonization to regard their own knowledge as less when compared to that of the colonizer" and the corresponding "loss of confidence in traditional methods, or controversy about what these methods truly are and who these methods serve."[18] To mitigate this effect, LeBaron recommends examining all such proposals to adopt indigenized western institutions by asking: "For whom do our processes work? How do our processes accommodate conversations about what is important, how it is important, and for whom? Whose values do our processes mirror and whose do they exclude?"[19]

This discussion is germane to deliberations about indigenizing the ombudsman institution. While it is true that the ombudsman institution is highly-adaptable—the institution is not culturally or ideologically neutral. The institution is imbued with the euro-american cultural framework in which it was conceived. By deconstructing the ombudsman institution to its essential elements, and evaluating these characteristics, we reveal the extent to which western culture pervades the institution. The ubiquitous characteristics of effective ombudsman institutions are published by the United Nations Centre for Human Rights, the United States Ombudsman Association, and the American Bar Association. I will evaluate these criteria to illustrate how they reflect western values and philosophy, and to demonstrate how these elements may run contrary to a First Nation's values, beliefs, and traditional practices. However, before proceeding, I should reinforce that my objective is to draw the attention of First Nation communities to the potential risk in adopting indigenized western institutions. It is also to encourage First Nation communities to identify their respective beliefs, values, and traditional practices, and to evaluate the values imported through western institutions in the light of the First Nation's own cultural perspective. Finally, my goal is to promote the development of dispute resolution machinery that is in harmony with the First Nation's distinct cultural identity, whether that be through establishing a First Nation ombudsman, through reviving traditional dispute resolution practices, or through an entirely unique institution. This article identifies ways in which the ombudsman institution *may* conflict with a First Nation's beliefs, values, and traditional practices—but it is for the First Nation itself to determine if the ombudsman institution is, in fact, appropriate within their cultural framework and if it meets their specific needs. Transplanting the institution into the aboriginal context in the absence of such consideration may result in considerable effort and finances being invested in an ineffective and impotent agency. Worse yet, it could result in entrenching euro-american values and ways of thinking and, in so doing, eclipsing a First Nation's traditional practices, contemporary culture, and aboriginal wisdom.

The Foundation

There is a danger in making generalizations concerning the values and beliefs of a particular culture. However, such generalizations are useful to the extent that they allow us to gain some perspective on the conceptual framework that informs our own point-of-view—especially those concepts that we believe are universally shared. One such concept is justice—and this is a foundational concept with respect to the ombudsman function. In the western mind, "justice is satisfied by appealing to a set of *principles and procedures* that can *neutrally* adjudicate between parties' rights and interests."[20] As this definition suggests, western culture's suspicion and distrust of authority and authority figures[21] pervades the western perception of justice. The need to fix or codify right-protective "principles and procedures" (e.g., *The Canadian Charter of Rights and Freedoms*) evidences the euro-american preoccupation with "protecting" rights and entitlements from the dominant authority—and is a prerequisite for the neutral adjudication process (which itself reveals this anxiety). Western culture's mistrust of authority and hierarchical power structures is also shown in the fact that political, social, and legal institutions are structured to balance power, level authority, and create a system of checks and balances. This anxiety is not shared by collectivists who, within their in-group, "are more comfortable than individualists in hierarchical structures."[22] However, the ombudsman institution is indivisible from this western anxiety. The United Nations, ombudsman associations, commentators, and others all insist that the ombudsman institution be entrenched in legislation. This criterion is so essential to the institution that it is an ubiquitous feature in its definition: "an office *provided for by the constitution or by action of the Legislature* and headed by an independent, high level public official who is *responsible to the Legislature or Parliament*"[23] and "a body which is established by a Government *under the constitution, or by law or decree.*"[24]

Neutrality is also essential to the ombudsman institution:

> In the dominant western political vocabulary, there is an easily available story about how to resolve disputes between groups over perceived conflicts of interests, aspirations, or access to resources: let each side make its case before a *neutral third party*, who will decide *objectively* on a just settlement.[25]

The importance of neutrality to the ombudsman institution is engendered by western culture's understanding of fairness—an understanding that is not universally shared. In the western mindset, decision-making power is legitimate only insofar as it is "objective," which means abstracted to the level of reason. For euro-american cultures, reason represents the height of validity and legitimacy. However, some have pointed out that setting "reason" as the benchmark requires

> *assimilation to standards that are not themselves neutral* but in fact represent the perspective of dominant social groups. When parties to disputes are asked to step away from their parochial interest and identities to recognize the demands of reason and fairness, they are actually being forced to conform to the hegemony of some similarly parochial set of standards: feminists have argued that these norms are masculine; critical race theorists, that they are based on historically specific understandings of white identity; and neo-Marxists that they continue to represent bourgeois interests as universal.[26]

Further, neutral decision-making cannot take place in a vacuum: it requires a pre-existing set of standards on which to base its decisions. The standard may be reason itself, or it may be a codified set of principles and procedures—regardless, both, as the foregoing discussion indicates, are invariably permeated with cultural values and norms. Consequently, a First Nation that shares the western perception of justice, and chooses to adopt the ombudsman institution, must be conscious of the standard of fairness and legality it sets for the institution. In fixing such standards, a First Nation must consider whose interests are being reinforced and whose values are being entrenched. Even if such standards do not reflect unshared western values, they may fail to recognize the heterogeneity and diverse needs within their own communities, thereby forcing vulnerable and marginalized groups (e.g., residential school survivors, women, or non-reserve members) to act within a framework that reflects only the needs and perspective of the already powerful.

Objectivity and reason are inseparable from the ombudsman institution, and, as elements of fairness and justice, are values not shared by many First Nation communities. In these communities, a "fair" dispute-resolution process is not dispassionate or cerebral. Elmer Ghostkeeper describes how "over time, science has repressed wisdom derived from personal learning experiences and connection with nature. Science has difficulty measuring things that cannot be quantified. It cannot quantify the spirit, emotion, and personal experiences with nature."[27] He juxtaposes this with Cree aboriginal wisdom that values the four aspects of self: a belief system that does not simply legitimize the cerebral, but believes the emotional, physical, and spiritual aspects to be equally important.[28] Among Australia's aboriginal peoples, emotion has a vital role in dispute resolution: "In grievances between individuals, aggrieved parties were given the chance to express the way they felt—even through shouting, yelling, and screaming. Open displays of anger were seen as part of the resolution process."[29] Clearly, the western idealization of objectivity, that abstracts conflict situations out of their particular factual and emotional context to frame the dispute in the language of reason, is inconsonant with the values and beliefs of some aboriginal cultures.

One could respond to this analysis by proposing that the simple solution is to indigenize the institution at this fundamental level: by simply replacing the above-described western orientations of justice, fairness, and legality with aboriginal conceptions of the same. In this way, First Nations can adopt an institution that is devoid of western influence. In my view, this cannot be achieved in this manner. Although the ombudsman institution has become very diverse over a history of being re-interpreted by different cultures and adapted to fit new environments, it has a core that cannot be altered without directly impacting its effectiveness—and this core is inseparable from western values. The United Nations[30] and several other credible organizations[31] have isolated these core or essential characteristics either in the context of model ombudsman legislation or as recommendations for establishing or developing effective ombudsman institutions. The United Nations criteria differs slightly from the others in that the requirements are considered essential to all national human rights institutions, including human rights commissions, the hybrid human rights ombudsman, and specialized commissions.[32] The others are specific to the ombudsman institution. Interestingly, they differ slightly in terms of the weight attached to the particular effectiveness factors—but, importantly, are largely the same. Chief Roberta Jamieson highlights the same criteria and describes them as "fundamental characteristics" of a First Nations ombudsman—further substantiating their indivisibility from the institution, even in the First Nation context. As the essential criteria outlined by ombudsman organizations and the United Nations overlap and intersect at various points, I use the *United States Ombudsman Association Model Act* (2003)[33] as a starting point and incorporate additional factors from the United Nations document as we move through the analysis.

The *United States Ombudsman Association Model Act* pares the essential criteria for an effective ombudsman institution down to four criteria: independence, impartiality, confidentiality, and a credible review process. Unquestionably, these criteria are essential if the institution is to gain the trust of both the administration and the public. But the "public" to whom this appeals has a euro-american conceptual orientation and a western understanding of justice.

Independence

Independence in the ombudsman context means: "free from outside control and influence. This standard enables the Ombudsman to function as an impartial and critical entity that reports findings and makes recommendations based solely on a review of facts and law, in the light of reason and fairness."[34] As is obvious from this definition, the value placed on the independence of the institution is indistinguishable from the premium placed on objectivity. Although independence as a concept is not necessarily incongruent with aboriginal wisdom, the emphasis placed on it reinforces western, and not necessarily aboriginal, notions of credibility. The western distrust of authority figures means that the ombudsman must be perceived as cocooned from all influence, except that of reason. This relationship between independence and credibility is evidenced by the United States Ombudsman Association's assertion that "[t]o be credible and effective, the office of the ombuds is independent in its structure, function, and appearance."[35] Aboriginal notions of credibility may be more oriented towards natural authority within the community, personal experience, or eldership.

The emphasis on independence also manifests modern industrialized society's philosophy that "conflict can be 'managed,'" resulting in a dispute resolution philosophy that believes that "[b]y concentrating on reaching agreement among parties "at the table" a conflict situation is conceptualized as something that can be acted on and changed in isolation from any larger surrounding context.... humans can subject phenomena around them to "rational", "routinized" controls. The structure "facilitated" by a third party is such a control."[36] Such a philosophy is discordant with that of some aboriginal cultures. First Nation leaders have described their values with respect to conflict as including: a holistic approach to life, cooperation, harmony, consensus decision making, privacy, the relativity of time, and spirituality.[37] These values are culturally dissonant with a myopic approach that pares "conflict" down to isolated "disputes" in an attempt to control conflict through its isolation from the broader context. The ombudsman institution is designed to simply manage *disputes*, not conflict as such—except as a corpus of individual disputes. This aspect of the ombudsman institution may be especially problematic in some First Nation communities where "[a]n issue may have been created in one situation because of an issue in another and so on back even into a previous generation. The persons in front of a conflict may not be the persons behind the conflict."[38] In this case, the institution's inability to consider conflict in the broader societal context would render the ombudsman institution ineffective in resolving disputes.

The premium placed on independence also results in a structural limitation of the institution. The American Bar Association states that: "[h]istorically, ombuds were created in parliamentary systems and were established in the constitution or by statute, appointed by the legislative body, and had a guarantee of independence from the control of any other officer, except for responsibility to the legislative body. This structure remains a model for ensuring independence."[39] Because the ombudsman is appointed by the legislative branch of government, complaints concerning the legislative branch or the policy-making branch of the executive branch are *ultra vires* the ombudsman function.[40] Advocates of the institution justify this limitation by highlighting that the legislative branch is one whose "actions are conspicuous and subject to public scrutiny, and whose tenure is subject to periodic popular review."[41] This may be a fair response. However, a First Nations community that needs an ombudsman to investigate electoral irregularities, unfair election practices, or inequitable policies in their communities must be aware that the ombudsman institution is structurally incapable of investigating such complaints.

This structural limitation may also be of special significance to aboriginal communities where there may be unclear delimitations of the different branches of government—or confusion as to roles and responsibilities. Chief Roberta Jamieson points out that "[b]ecause the role of Chiefs and Councils has been seen in the past as primarily an administrative one, even though they may have been elected to their positions, the line between public servant and elected official continues to be blurred today."[42] This imprecise delimitation of boundaries is made more problematic in smaller First Nations where "it may be that a "band manager" is the only person with sufficient authority to deal with the Ombudsman, or that all complaints have to go to Chief and Council."[43] Centuries of colonialization have also left the First Nation public, and the administration, confused about the respective roles of the federal government, administrative agencies, and band council: "There is a lack of clarity on the locus of responsibility. There is uncertainty of how to appeal, and to whom."[44] As a result, a prohibition on investigating the policy-making or legislative branch may be unworkable, or undesirable, in the First Nations context.

Impartiality

Impartiality is described as being "at the heart of the Ombudsman concept,"[45] as "[b]oth the complainant and the agency are able to place confidence in the Ombudsman knowing that the Ombudsman has no vested interest in the outcome of a complaint investigation."[46] In the western model, "ignorance and distance, that is anonymity, provide legitimate "rational-legal" authority, in the Weberian sense of having the "right" to exercise influence."[47] Authority requires that recommendations be that of an objective, neutral third party that scientifically sets out to "gather facts from relevant sources and apply relevant policies, guidelines, and laws"[48] and "does not allow personal views regarding the subject matter or the parties involved to affect decisions."[49] Western culture is distrustful of those who have an interest in outcomes; whereas, decision-makers that have "nothing to lose," that are dissociated from the social consequences of their decisions, may make some aboriginal cultures uneasy. For these cultures, the person chosen to be a decision-maker is often "an integral element maintaining the stability of the group life" as "[i]t is the human bond that establishes both trust and continuity through the process. Relationship to and knowledge of disputants and their social context provide legitimate "traditional" authority."[50] Consequently, these decision-makers are often chosen for their perceived wisdom, relationship to the parties, and/or personal experience—consequently, their personal views are expected and encouraged to inform their decisions.

In addition to being undesirable, impartiality, in the sense of being disinterested, may also be particularly difficult in the First Nations context. Impartiality is usually described as being free from the potential for or appearance of "conflict of interest." Chief Roberta Jamieson points out that such a requirement is complicated by

> relationships between families and neighbours, clans and nations. Roles and issues may not be quite as clear-cut in a First Nation setting—officials may be relatives or neighbours and disputes of family and neighbourhood may carry over into official business. There can be cross-disputes, where the same parties are official-client and client-official in a pair of disputes. In a First Nation setting, the public servant is not an anonymous figure, and will be seen by the "public" at the store, arena, or a weekend event on a regular basis.[51]

In the web of relationships within a First Nation community, the avoidance of conflict of interest required for impartiality can be difficult, or impossible. That is, apart from bringing in an outsider—and that solution may be unworkable in the context of a First Nation ombudsman. Chief Jamieson insists that a First Nation ombudsman must "know community issues, understand and be open to diversity, have the ability to be appropriately respectful to different clients in different ways and the ability to recognize and address bias and prejudice, as well as being able to communicate sensitively and interculturally."[52] It is unlikely that an outsider to the community could possess these characteristics to an adequate standard.

Confidentiality

Confidentiality is the "Ombudsman's tool"[53] or "an essential characteristic of ombuds that permits the process to work effectively. Confidentiality promotes disclosure from reluctant complainants, elicits candid discussions by all parties, and provides an increased level of protection against retaliation to or by any party."[54] However, confidentiality may be problematic or undesirable in the First Nation context. For the reasons that Chief Jamieson set out above, true confidentiality may be an impossible criterion in the web of relationships and the proximity of association in many aboriginal communities. Moreover, confidentiality prevents interpersonal communication between parties. The neutral third party either appropriates the parties' voices to shuttle expression between parties or there is no expression between parties at all, with the decision-maker acting as a sponge for expression. In the aboriginal context this may pose special problems. Some commentators theorize that, "[f]or collectivists, communication tends to be associative. This means that much more attention is paid to the context of the communication, including verbal associations, gestures, body posture and the facial muscles of the other person."[55] If this is accurate, confidentiality will impede effective communication in some aboriginal contexts.

Of course, the criteria of confidentiality may be completely compatible with a First Nation's values. Where, for example, a First Nation values an impartial investigation and recommendation from an authoritative, neutral third party—confidentiality is likely desirable, especially to the extent that it circumvents any fears associated with retaliation. In fact, assurances of confidentiality in eliciting public concerns may be particularly valuable in collectivist cultures, as some collectivists are "uncomfortable with assertion if it may mean that other members of the in-group lose face or are subjected to public criticism."[56] However, in those First Nation communities that value reconciliation and healing, confidentiality is impractical. Although not universally true of aboriginal peoples, some claim that: "[n]ative peoples are consensus oriented. Elders are not unilateral decision-makers. There is an emphasis on solving the immediate dispute, but also rebuilding the relationship that existed before the dispute. This healing focus is integral to the dispute resolution process in many native cultures."[57] Where healing is the desired outcome, parties would need to convene in some meaningful way to express views, recognize interests, and arrive at a harmonious result. Confidentiality would not be amenable to such an outcome.

Credible Review Process

This criterion immediately brings into question the indicators of "credibility" in a particular cultural framework. As already explored in detail, credibility in the dispute resolution context is inseparable from objectivity and neutrality, and the associated appeal to a fixed set of standards. The indicators of "credibility" under this essential characteristic reflect this orientation. For example,

- "The Ombudsman should be qualified to analyze issues and matters of law, administration, and policy."[58]

- "The Ombudsman's jurisdiction should be clearly defined and the Ombudsman should not act outside of that jurisdiction."[59]

- "The Ombudsman should have sufficient powers to conduct thorough investigations."[60]

- "The process for how complaints are to be made, received, and acted upon, including the scope and manner of investigations should be defined and transparent."[61]

- "The Ombudsman should, at least annually, report generally on the activities of the office to the Ombudsman's appointing authority, other policy makers, and the public."[62]

In contrast, indicators of credibility in the aboriginal context may focus more on the credibility of the decision-maker and less on the credibility of the process. In the result, a "credible" review process is one where the decision-maker utilizes the characteristics that vest her with authority: for example, knowledge of traditional practices, spiritual insight, an understanding of the community, or respected life experience. In others, a credible review process may be one that respects traditional practices, like consulting with elders prior to making a decision. In all, neither objectivity nor neutrality is relevant to the credibility of the process.

It must also be noted that, in the western mindset, the "credibility" of the review process is associated with the institution's coercive power. The ombudsman's recommendations do not have binding force; however, the ombudsman may report the administration's reluctance to implement her recommendations to the legislative branch, which is in turn meant to compel the responsible minister to make the recommended change. If the legislative branch is unresponsive, the ombudsman can report the legislature's apathy to the electorate—which can put pressure on the legislative branch to implement the recommendations. Such power is essential to the credibility of the institution in the minds of the western public. Professor Reif states that "the populace served by the institution must perceive that the institution can provide it with real benefits: through its right to complain about poor administration or human rights breaches, to obtain an impartial investigation of the matter, and to have some positive results if wrongdoing is found."[63] Having "some positive results" invariably means having some power to induce change and some ability to exert control—however limited. For this reason, the United Nations includes in its essential characteristics a "defined jurisdiction and adequate powers," stating that "[p]ower, in this context, refers to the ability of a national institution to perform a certain act or to compel such performance by an individual or other entity. Power must be enforceable."[64] For this reason, most western commentators are almost apologetic about the lack of enforcement power behind the ombudsman's decisions and are quick to point out that there is some measure of coercive power in the "'soft' powers of persuasion and the ability to publicize, including when the government fails to implement recommendations made."[65]

In some aboriginal cultures, the credibility of the review process is not related to control or coercive power. The credibility of the process may be solely dependent on the respect the decision-maker has in the community. Or perhaps the credibility is related to the extent to which the process is reconcilable with traditional practices, such as consulting elders. In yet others, the credibility of the process in the public perception may also, like the ombudsman institution, be inseparable from its outcome—however, in the aboriginal context, the outcome may be the healing of the community or the reconciliation of disputing parties. In this way, the ombudsman institution's structural orientation toward the "soft" enforcement of its recommendations may be irreconcilable with aboriginal values, traditional practices, and desired outcomes.

Other Essential Criteria

The United Nations provides some additional criteria that it considers essential to the ombudsman institution: accessibility, cooperation, operational efficiency, and accountability. Accessibility involves both public awareness of the institution and social and physical accessibility.[66] This criterion is equally essential to the machinery of dispute resolution in First Nation communities, regardless of what form it takes. A special challenge for a First Nation dispute resolution mechanism is that their subjects may live off-reserve, be marginalized by mental health issues caused by a residential school experience, or be geographically isolated. To ameliorate this difficulty, Chief Jamieson recommends the use of intake clinics which allows the dispute resolution machinery to reach out to assist and educate those that, for a variety of reasons, may find it difficult to access its services.[67]

Cooperation with non-governmental organizations, other national institutions, and intergovernmental organizations is also considered essential.[68] Professor Reif would add to this the importance of government cooperation: "political and government support must be given to the institution, its work, and its recommendations. A responsive government in the positive sense is crucial to the effectiveness of a national human rights institution."[69] Cooperation among First Nations that share a similar cultural identity may be valuable in terms of communicating effective solutions and shared challenges. Also, a First Nation may find non-governmental organizations (such as the Institute for the Advancement of Aboriginal Women and the Residential School Survivors Healing Centre) valuable in that they can draw attention to the special concerns of vulnerable persons within the community, support the First Nation in being responsive to any unique needs, and assist marginalized groups in bringing forward a dispute.

Operational efficiency includes adequate resources, effective working methods, personnel matters, and review and evaluation of internal processes.[70] Operational efficiency is also important to First Nation institutions; however, again, the interpretation of what it means to be "efficient" may differ between aboriginal and western cultures. Relevantly, the personal traits of the ombudsman and staff are included under "personnel matters" as a sub-factor of effectiveness. Professor Reif would argue that this factor is essential:

> It is extremely important to appoint an individual or individuals to head a national human rights institution who have expertise, integrity, and credibility in the eyes of both the government and the populace. The strength of character and, occasionally, the courage needed to operate an effective national human rights institution should not be underestimated. In both democratizing states and established democracies, a strong, competent, and credible commission, ombudsman, or human rights ombudsman can be the determining factor in the effectiveness of the institution.[71]

In many aboriginal cultures, the individual qualities of the decision-maker(s) are essential to the effectiveness of the dispute resolution machinery—not relegated to virtual inconsequence as they are in the ombudsman paradigm. As quoted earlier in this article, Chief Jamieson notes the crucial importance of the personal qualities of a First Nation ombudsman and outlines the qualities that an effective ombudsman must possess. In some aboriginal communities, the personal qualities of the decision-maker may be what imbue her with natural authority and her recommendations with respect—and, consequently, may be a vital factor in the

First Nation context. Finally, accountability refers to the ombudsman's legal and financial accountability to the government and to the public it serves.[72] In the western context, this "essential" criterion is met through the ombudsman's annual reporting obligation to government and its ability to issue public reports. However, the premium that western culture places on the written word is not shared by all First Nation communities—many of which were founded on, and continue in, the oral tradition. Moreover, the "essentialness" of accountability is associated with the western distrust of power: even the ombudsman must be answerable to ensure that she too does not overstep her defined jurisdiction. Apart from these concerns, it may be valuable for a First Nation ombudsman to periodically hold public meetings to discuss the corpus of the community's concerns, her stated recommendations, and the outcome of relevant disputes. Such meetings may assist in highlighting areas of significant public concern and give the public an opportunity to voice suggestions for improving the efficiency and effectiveness of the institution.

The Way Forward

All of the foregoing leads us back to the initial question: Should a First Nation establish an ombudsman on reserves? I cannot answer that question. Chief Robert Yazzie (Chief Justice of the Navajo Nation) explains:

> When designing effective dispute resolution mechanisms, one cannot simply look at a method or procedure for doing things, write down a checklist of what to do, and implement it anywhere. We did two very important things when we revived peacemaking. First, we looked at Navajo values and thinking. Second, we identified the traditional Navajo procedure and the leaders who use it. Those are Navajo-specific cultural values. If your community wants to revive effective indigenous dispute resolution practices, it must engage in a similar process. Each of you must ask yourself: What is the basis for my culture's ideas of right and wrong and how to do things?[73]

For the Navajo, this process lead them to a very successful form of dispute resolution called "peacemaking":

> Traditional Navajo civil leadership is based upon the (often informal) selection of individuals as leaders who have proven themselves to be successful in speaking, planning, and in spirituality. They are leaders whom the people listen to when discussing a community dispute. The civil leader

90

or *naat'aanii* will call people together when there is a dispute so they can "talk it out." This process involves prayer, to commit people to serious and respectful discussion of the dispute; recounting the facts of the dispute (actual and perceived, including opinions about the facts and the emotional impact of what happened); teachings of traditional approaches to the problem by the *naat'aanii*, plans for future action, and finally, a consensus decision by the group.[74]

Recognizing the challenges posed by reviving traditional practices when a First Nation's cultural identity is often a "blend of Western and indigenous ideas of law and conflict," the Navajo approach was to "bring traditional values back into contemporary life *not to replace contemporary life*; to assist offenders, victims, and others to resolve internal psychological and spiritual conflict; and to reach an effective balance of the sacred and contemporary in healing communities and resolving disputes."[75]

The need to strike a balance between contemporary life and traditional practices has been universally recognized in First Nation communities—but the "right" balance is unique to the community itself. To honour a tradition that valued consensus decision-making and consultation, the Métis Settlements proposed the establishment of an Elders Committee, appointed by settlement government, that would "hear appeals of controversial government decisions, have power to resolve disputes within delegated areas of jurisdiction (such as land and membership), and advise settlement government on other controversial issues."[76] Community participation in the enactment of settlement by-laws and policymaking would incorporate the traditional values of consensus decision-making and consultation into the process.[77] Also, the proposal provided that Elders Committee decisions could be appealed to a Métis arbitrator or a Métis arbitration panel.[78] Whether such a model would have been effective remains unknown, however, as the model was subsequently altered to accommodate disputes with non-Métis persons (especially in the areas of membership and oil and gas rights and revenues).[79] The final result was the successful Métis Settlements Appeal Tribunal (MSAT) in which

> [t]he emphasis on creating specific roles for elders gave way to the inclusion of elders through vehicles such as alternative dispute resolution processes promoted by MSAT, appointments to MSAT, participation in general community consultations on settlement laws, and expert advice on matters such as Métis ancestry and traditional land-use practices. Elder opinion is also viewed as important evidence by MSAT in the assessment of the cultural impact of resource development on Métis land, the resolution of

family and estate matters, and identification of traditional Métis practices relevant to the resolution of contemporary disputes.[80]

In spite of the above functions, the role of Elders in the dispute resolution process has unfortunately diminished from its traditional importance.[81] To remedy this, mediation is contemplated as a means of revitalizing the Elders' traditional role in dispute resolution.[82] The mediation model being considered for the Métis Settlements would revive the Cree belief system of a Medicine Wheel: a mediator assists the disputing parties in working through four stages: "hearing your voice (telling your story), finding yourself (what do you see & hear & feel), finding balance & understanding (discovering a place of respect), and opening your heart (creating a place where healing can happen)."[83]

For the Tsuu T'ina, creating an effective dispute resolution process required an acknowledgement that the Tsuu T'ina "live in both cultures" and "that the clock cannot be turned back completely."[84] The Tsuu T'ina recognized that they shared some values relevant to justice with western culture, such as "independence, neutrality, knowledge (cultural and legal) and impartiality in decision making."[85] Therefore, for their community, an effective dispute resolution mechanism involved establishing a court that maps the traditional values of "healing and restoration" onto a western judicial model.[86] The two sets of values are balanced by appointing a judge that has "an innate understanding of the cultural sensibilities of First Nations people through direct personal involvement with the culture, [has] resided on a reserve and [has] worked with Aboriginal people."[87] The Tsuu T'ina responded to community concerns respecting "impartiality, legal education, and independence of the judiciary" by recommending that the judge be a "highly qualified member of the First Nations Bar from outside the Treaty 7 area to avoid community pressure and to set the tone of 'non-interference'"[88]

For First Nations, like the Tsuu T'ina, that share the western conception of justice, establishing an ombudsman on reserves may be appropriate. The Mohawk First Nation has established a successful First Nation Ombudsman at Kahnawake.[89] A Métis Settlements Ombudsman, funded by the Alberta government, was created in 2003 by the Minister of Aboriginal Affairs and Northern Development to resolve disputes concerning Métis Settlements management and leadership.[90] The office's mission is to "promote the rights and responsibilities of Métis Settlement Councils, staff, businesses operated by Councils, and members, through inspections, investigations, and recommendations."[91] Disputes are resolved through discussion and mediation and, where these processes fail, through the impartial investigation and recommendation of the ombudsman. Anyone may make a complaint to the Métis Settlements Ombudsman; however, like most ombudsman institutions, complainants must have made their own attempts to solve the dispute and have first exhausted all other available means of appeal. Like all classical ombudsman, the Métis Settlements Ombudsman must report its activities to the legislature.

Conclusion

As evidenced by the foregoing, surveying traditional beliefs and practices and identifying contemporary values have lead First Nation communities to diverse models for effectively meeting their dispute resolution needs. There is no "right" model. Each First Nation must establish a model that embraces their cultural identity, recognizes contemporary challenges, and is responsive to the special needs of the vulnerable or marginalized members of their communities. For some communities, such introspection will lead them to the ombudsman institution. For others, self-assessment will show the institution's inherent values to be discordant with the community's closely-held beliefs and practices. Regardless, First Nation communities cannot avoid embarking on a course of "[r]econciling our memories in order to re-envision our future"[92]—as only through a process of retrospection and introspection can communities perceive the best way forward.

Endnotes

1. Edward Twitchell Hall, *The Silent Language* (New York: Anchor Books, 1973) at 30.

2. *Infra* notes 4 and 5.

3. Roberta L. Jamieson, "The First Nation Ombudsman" (Prepared for a Symposium on Specialized Tribunals and First Nations Legal Institutions, Radisson Saskatoon Hotel, May 29-31, 2002) [unpublished].

4. Section 11(1) prescribes that "[t]he council of a band shall, by band law, authorize an impartial person or body to consider fairly and expeditiously any complaint by a member of the band or a resident of the reserve (a) alleging the contravention or the unfair or improper application - by the council, a member of the council or an employee of the band - of this *Act*, a code, regulations made under section 32 or a band law made under section 18; or (b) contesting any decision made - by the council, a member of the council or an employee of the band - against the member of the band or resident of the reserve in the exercise of a discretionary power" Bill C-7, *The First Nations Governance Act*, 2nd Sess., 37th Parl., 2002, (1st reading October 9, 2002 as amended by the Standing Committee on Aboriginal Affairs, Northern Development and Natural Resources).

5.   Bill C-399, *An Act to establish a First Nations Ombudsman and a First Nations Auditor to assist with administrative and financial problems*, 1st Sess., 37th Parl., 2001 (1st reading September 28, 2001); Bill C-222, *An Act to establish the office of First Nations Ombudsman to investigate complaints relating to administrative and communication problems between members of First Nations communities and their First Nation and between First Nations, allegations of improper financial administration and allegations of electoral irregularities*, 2nd Sess., 36th Parl., 1999 (1st reading October 15, 1999).

6.   *Supra* note 3.

7.   United Nations Centre for Human Rights (UNCHR). *National Human Rights Institutions: A Handbook on the Establishment and Strengthening of National Institutions for the Promotion and Protection of Human Rights, Professional Training Series No. 4.* UN Doc. HR/P/PT/4, UN Sales No. E.95.XIV.2 (Geneva: Centre for Human Rights, 1995).

8.   United States Ombudsman Association, "Draft Governmental Ombudsman Standards" (June 2003), online: United States Ombudsman Association <http://www.usombudsman.org/ DraftSTANDARDS.PDF> (date accessed: September 2, 2004).

9.   American Bar Association, "Standards approved by the ABA House of Delegates at the 2001 Annual Meeting" (2001), online: American Bar Association <http://ww.abanet.org/adminlaw/approvedreport.doc> (date accessed: September 2, 2004).

10.   The Ombudsman Association, "Code of Ethics and Standards of Practice," online: The Ombudsman Association <http://www.ombuds-toa.org/downloads/TOA%20code-sop.pdf> (date accessed: September 2, 2004).

11.   Ngaire Woods, "Good Governance in International Organizations" (1999) 5 Global Governance 39, cited by Linda C. Reif, "Building Democratic Institutions: The Role of National Human Rights Institutions in Good Governance and Human Rights Protection" (2000) 13 Harv. Hum. Rts. J. 1 at 16.

12.   Woods, *ibid* at 44.

13.   Reif, *supra* note 11 at 16.

14.   *Ibid.* at 24.

15.   United States Ombudsman Association, "Model Ombudsman Act
       For State Governments" (February 1997) at 4, online: United
       States Ombudsman Association
       <http://www.usombudsman.org/References/modelombudact.htm>
       (date accessed: September 2, 2004).

16.   For a very interesting theory that the clear objective of the
       government in establishing such institutions is to "neutralize conflict
       that could threaten state or capital…. by responding to grievances in
       ways that inhibit their transformation into serious challenges to the
       domination of state and capital" see: Richard L. Abel, "The
       Contradictions of Informal Justice" in Richard L. Abel, ed., *The
       Politics of Informal Justice: The American Experience* vol. 1 (New
       York: Academic Press, 1982) 267 at 280. Abel argues that "[b]oth
       state and capital create informal institutions so that they can retain
       control over the handling of those grievances that escape the purview
       of formal institutions and can continue to influence: which complaints
       get aired, by whom, to whom, in what form and forum, how they are
       processed, and what remedy is granted. All these institutions are
       created and controlled by *respondents*, never by the grievants
       themselves."

17.   Michelle LeBaron, "Learning New Dances: Finding Effective Ways
       to Address Intercultural Disputes" in Catherine Bell & David
       Kahane, eds., *Intercultural Dispute Resolution in Aboriginal
       Contexts: Canadian and International Perspectives* (Vancouver:
       UBC Press, 2004) 11 at 23.

18.   *Ibid.*

19.   *Ibid.* at 26.

20.   David Kahane, "What is Culture? Generalizing about Aboriginal and
       New Comer Perspectives" in Catherine Bell & David Kahane, eds.,
       *Intercultural Dispute Resolution in Aboriginal Contexts: Canadian
       and International Perspectives* (Vancouver: UBC Press, 2004) 28 at
       29 [emphasis mine].

21.   Michelle LeBaron Duryea, *Conflict and Culture: A Literature Review and Bibliography* (Victoria: UVic Institute for Dispute Resolution, 1992) at 49, referring to Harry C. Triandis, Robert Bontempo & Marcelo J. Villareal, "Individualism and Collectivism: Cross-Cultural Perspectives on Self-Ingroup Relationships" (1988) 54:2 Journal of Personality and Social Psychology 323-38.

22.   Lebaron Duryea, *ibid.* at 41, referring to Harry C. Triandis, "Theoretical Concepts that are Applicable to an Analysis of Ethnocentrism" in Richard Brislin, ed., *Applied Cross-Cultural Psychology* (Newbury Park, Calif: Sage Publications, 1990).

23.   International Bar Association in a resolution passed in Vancouver in 1974 [emphasis mine].

24.   *Supra* note 7 at 6 [emphasis mine].

25.   *Supra* note 20 [emphasis mine].

26.   *Ibid.* at 30-31.

27.   Elmer Ghostkeeper, "*Weche* Teachings: Aboriginal Wisdom and Dispute Resolution" in Catherine Bell & David Kahane, eds., *Intercultural Dispute Resolution in Aboriginal Contexts: Canadian and International Perspectives* (Vancouver: UBC Press, 2004) 161 at 165.

28.   *Ibid.*

29.   Larissa Behrendt, "Cultural Conflict in Colonial Legal Systems: an Australian Perspective" in Catherine Bell & David Kahane, eds., *Intercultural Dispute Resolution in Aboriginal Contexts: Canadian and International Perspectives* (Vancouver: UBC Press, 2004) 116 at 123.

30.   United Nations Centre for Human Rights (UNCHR), *supra* note 7.

31.   *Supra* note 8; *supra* note 15; United States Ombudsman Association, "Public Sector Ombudsman" (2003), online: United States Ombudsman Association <http://www.usombudsman.org/References /publicsectorombudsman.htm> (date accessed: September 2, 2004); *supra* note 9.

32. Seeking to advance the international communities' commitment to the inherent value and equality of each human being, the United Nations enacted the *Universal Declaration of Human Rights* and has actively promoted the establishment of national human rights institutions to assist in implementing its principles. National human rights institutions may be broadly classified as: the ombudsman, human rights commissions, and specialized commissions. The ombudsman's primary function is to ensure accountability within the public administration—human rights commissions and specialized commissions focus more generally on human rights violations, like discrimination, in both the private and public sector. The shared goal is to ensure that human rights are protected within the various political, social, and economic power structures.

33. *Supra* note 8.

34. *Ibid.* at 1.

35. *Supra* note 9 at 5.

36. Lederach, *supra* note 1 at 27.

37. LeBaron Duryea, *supra* note 21 at 35-56, referring to Marg Huber, "Canada Focus: Mediation Through the Eyes of Native Peoples" (1991) 4:1 Cultural Diversity at Work 6 [emphasis mine].

38. *Supra* note 3 at 16.

39. *Supra* note 9 at 5.

40. *Supra* note 8 at 10; Reif, *supra* note 11 at 7.

41. "Draft Governmental Ombudsman Standards," *ibid.*

42. *Supra* note 3 at 16.

43. *Ibid.* at 17.

44. *Ibid.* at 16.

45. *Supra* note 8 at 6.

46. *Ibid.*

47. Lederach, *supra* note 1 at 25, referring to Max Weber, *The Theory of Social and Economic Organization* (New York: Oxford University Press, 1947).

48. *Supra* note 9 at 6.

49. *Supra* note 8 at 7.

50. Lederach, *supra* note 1 at 25-26, referring to Max Weber, *The Theory of Social and Economic Organization* (New York: Oxford University Press, 1947).

51. *Supra* note 3 at 16.

52. *Ibid.*

53. *Supra* note 8 at 7.

54. *Supra* note 9 at 7.

55. LeBaron Duryea, *supra* note 21 at 40, referring to Harry C. Triandis, "Theoretical Concepts that are Applicable to an Analysis of Ethnocentrism" in Richard Brislin, ed., *Applied Cross-Cultural Psychology* (Newbury Park, Calif: Sage, 1990).

56. *Supra* note 21 at 48.

57. *Ibid.* at 12, referring to Barbara Deane, "Conflict in Multicultural Contexts: What We Know—What We Don't Know" (1991) 4:1 Cultural Diversity at Work 10-11.

58. *Supra* note 8 at 9.

59. *Ibid.* at 10.

60. *Ibid.* at 11.

61. *Ibid.* at 12.

62. *Ibid.* at 13.

63.   Reif, *supra* note 11 at 27-28.

64.   *Supra* note 7 at 13.

65.   Reif, *supra* note 11 at 9.

66.   *Supra* note 7 at 13.

67.   *Supra* note 3 at 18.

68.   *Ibid.*

69.   Reif, *supra* note 11 at 27.

70.   *Supra* note 7 at 15.

71.   Reif, *supra* note 11 at 27.

72.   *Ibid.* at 17.

73.   Robert Yazzie (the Honourable Chief Justice of the Najavo Nation), "Navajo Peacemaking and Intercultural Dispute Resolution" in Catherine Bell & David Kahane, eds., *Interncultural Dispute Resolution* in *Aboriginal Contexts: Canadian International Perspectives* (Vancouver: UBC Press, 2004) 107 at 110.

74.   *Ibid.* at 149.

75.   Catherine Bell, "Indigenous Dispute Resolution Systems within Non-Indigenous Frameworks" in Catherine Bell & David Kahane, eds., *Intercultural Dispute Resolution in Aboriginal Contexts: Canadian and International Perspectives* (Vancouver: UBC Press, 2004) 241 at 246-247.

76.   Bell, *ibid.* at 249.

77.   *Ibid.*

78.   *Ibid.*

79.   *Ibid.*

80.   *Ibid.*

81.   *Ibid.* at 250.

82.   *Ibid.*

83.   *Ibid.* at 262, reproducing the work of Cathy Sveen & MSAT, "Healing Mediation Process" (presentation to MSAT Mediation Workshop, Edmonton, Alberta, 15 November 1997) [unpublished] as reproduced in Catherine Bell and MSAT, *Contemporary Métis Justice: The Settlement Way* (Saskatoon: Native Law Centre, 1999) at 110.

84.   Bell, *ibid.* at 251, quoting Marsha Erb, "The Tsuu T'ina Nation Proposal for a First Nation Court" (First Nations Justice Conference: Journey Towards Change, Yellowhead Tribal Council, Edmonton, Alberta, 10 November 1999) [unpublished].

85.   Bell, *ibid.*

86.   *Ibid.*

87.   *Ibid.* at 252., quoting the Alberta Justice Ministry, *A New Direction: Report of the Review Team Established to Study the Tsuu T'ina Nations Proposal for a First Nation Court* (Edmonton: Alberta Justice Communications, October 1998) at 27.

88.   *Ibid.* at 10.

89.   Greg Horn, "Kahnawake to set up Ombudsman Office" 8:14 Eastern Door (April 30,1999), online: Eastern Door <http://www.easterndoor.com/VOL. 8/8-14.htm#story4> (date accessed: September 2,2004).

90.   Office of the Métis Settlements Ombudsman, online: <http://www.metisombudsman.ab.ca>.

91.   *Ibid.*

92.   N. Bruce Duthu, "Commentary: Reconciling Our Memories in Order to Re-Envision our Future" in Catherine Bell & David Kahane, eds., *Intercultural Dispute Resolution in Aboriginal Contexts: Canadian*

and International Perspectives (Vancouver: UBC) 232 at 232, paraphrasing the ideas of Val Napolean, "Who Gets to Say What Happened? Reconciliation Issues for the Gitsan" in Catherine Bell & David Kahane, eds., *Intercultural Dispute Resolution in Aboriginal Contexts: Canadian and International Perspectives* (Vancouver: UBC) 176.

DEMONSTRATING YOUR VALUE

André Marin*

Nous vivons dans une époque qui met l'accent sur l'obtention de résultats, et la viabilité d'un bureau de l'ombudsman dépend de sa capacité à prouver sa valeur aux personnes qui bénéficient de ses services et à la population en général. Les ombudsmans ne devraient donc pas seulement souligner l'utilité de leur travail dans des cas «de cause à effet», c'est-à-dire ceux où leur intervention a un lien direct avec les résultats positifs obtenus. Ils devraient également reconnaître la valeur de cas moins évidents: par exemple, ceux où aucune amélioration n'aurait eu lieu s'ils ne s'étaient pas occupés de ce cas, et ce, même s'ils n'ont pas émis de recommandation à ce sujet. Cet article propose des listes de contrôle pouvant aider les ombudsmans à mieux déterminer la valeur de leur contribution au sujet de questions spécifiques ou systémiques, contribution qui dépasse le seul résultat évident d'avoir redressé un tort. L'emploi judicieux d'outils de contrôle de ce genre peut faciliter l'évaluation de la valeur de vos services.

****

En esta época en que se hace hincapié en la efectividad y los resultados, la viabilidad de la oficina del ombudsman depende de que el ombudsman pueda probar su valor a los interesados en su cometido y a la clientela. El ombudsman no debiera destacar su contribución solamente en los casos de 'causa y efecto', en

* Ombudsman, Ontario. Formerly, Ombudsman (June 1998-March 2005) of National Defence and Canadian Forces Ombudsman, Ottawa, Canada. This paper was based on a presentation at the 2003 United States Ombudsman Association (USOA) Conference, Hawaii.

los cuales los resultados positivos están inextricablemente ligados a su intervención. El valor de los casos sutiles de 'si no hubiese sido por' deberían también ser reconocidos, en los cuales el cambio no hubiese ocurrido de no haber intervenido el ombudsman, aún cuando no se hubiese realizado ninguna recomendación. Se brindan listas de control que el ombudsman puede tener en cuenta, con el fin de determinar si su contribución para solucionar un problema individual o sistémico podría demostrar ser de valor más allá de los obvios beneficios de la resolución de la queja. El uso juicioso de herramientas que den a conocer la labor del ombudsman en la comunidad es una parte vital para demostrar de manera efectiva el valor de su labor.

Introduction

Successful professionals at times credit their achievements to "doing the right thing". Doing the right thing is evidently a good beginning on the route to success. Nonetheless, the successful ombudsman will need to develop solid strategies in order to succeed in promoting change in an organization. Demonstrating your value will be one of the areas you will need to target your strategies.

This paper will summarize the experiences of the first five years of Canada's military Ombudsman in demonstrating value to its stakeholders. It will also set out some strategies for selling the value of your work.

While selling your work's value is a corollary to doing the actual work, if your constituents are not sold on the value-added nature of your enterprise, support for your office will dwindle and success will prove elusive.

What It Means

It may be useful at the outset to define what is meant by a *demonstration* of *value*. First, let us look at the *demonstration* aspect. In an ombudsman intervention, the best *demonstration* of value is twofold: the complainant and the organization are satisfied with the results you were able to bring to the case and the organization complained against acknowledges that your recommendations are warranted. Results usually mean the correction of an injustice. Unless the original demonstration is publicized to third parties, the matter ends there.

Second, let us look at the concept of *value*. In an instance where the complainant's result is a monetary award, the demonstration of the *value* is easy to ascertain. The work of the ombudsman, however, extends much further than monetary concepts.

It rests in repairing injustices or, as the mandate of the military Ombudsman states, to "contribute to substantial and long-lasting improvements in the welfare",[1] of its constituents. Value, in this sense, encompasses notions of usefulness and worth in favour of stakeholders.

This leads us to the question: Who are the vested stakeholders? To answer that question, ask yourself: Who has an interest in the outcome of the work you do?" Private sector or corporate ombudsman stakeholders may include the corporation, its shareholders, its managers, its clients, or its employees. Public sector ombudsmen have an even larger pool of stakeholders, extending to members of the public.

But once again, without publicizing the value-added aspect of the ombudsman, his contributions remain a narrow demonstration of value between the complainant, the organization being overseen, and the ombudsman, leaving other stakeholders out of the equation.

To truly demonstrate value in a meaningful way, it is incumbent upon the ombudsman's office to develop strategies that will reach out beyond the immediate parties. Without those strategies, the office is doomed to become a "best kept secret", which, as you will see below, can only spell bad news for the office.

Why Do It?

If you do the "right thing", and you know you are doing the "right thing", why be concerned about proving to others that you are a valuable asset? Will the truth not speak for itself? The answer is no.

First, although we like to think of ourselves as ultimately advancing the cause of justice, we currently live in an era of bottom lines. It has been said many times that one cannot put a price on justice, the implication being that justice is too elusive or intangible a concept to calculate mathematically. The reality is that this has not stopped society from trying to do so. Whether philosophically right or wrong, the viability of the ombudsman's office depends on it being able to prove its value. Demonstrating the *financial value* of the ombudsman's office is key to demonstrating *your* value.

Second, far from being a simple exercise in self-promotion, demonstrating your value is key to improving service to your clientele. If your office is effective and productive in resolving disputes and this message is communicated well to your stakeholders, you will develop the reputation of being an effective agent of change. With such a reputation, the ombudsman's office will be seen as a force to be reckoned with. When the ombudsman takes up matters which, in his opinion, are problematic, he will be much more likely to elicit a favourable response from the organization, both in terms of getting cooperation and changing the course of action to resolve matters. Undoubtedly, the office will also benefit from an enhanced standing and credibility in the eyes of complainants.

How to Do It

Because demonstrating your value is a pivotal factor contributing to your success, it is important never to miss an opportunity to showcase your contributions.

There will be cases, referred to here as *cause and effect* cases, where the complainant benefits from results that are inextricably tied to the involvement of the ombudsman's office. For example, if the office makes recommendations, either informally or in the more structured form of a report, which the organization accepts and implements, the causation between the change and the involvement of the ombudsman will not be up for debate. There may be other cases, *but for* cases, where the momentum for change is subtle and cannot be pinpointed with the same accuracy as when it is emanating directly from the ombudsman's initiative. The development of a strategy for demonstrating your value will be different depending on whether or not a change in the organization can be clearly traced back to the action of the ombudsman. Below are some suggestions on how to do this, beginning with the subtler *but for* situations.

"But For" Cases

There are cases that, *but for* the involvement of the ombudsman, would have never been resolved, even though he never made a single recommendation. These cases are distinguished from other cases where a change occurs to comply with an ombudsman recommendation.

The Dutch Armed Forces Inspector General once remarked to the military Ombudsman that he viewed his task as a "barometer, horsefly, oilcan and safety valve".[2] An ombudsman acting as a horsefly will nudge the organization to go in one way or another, without necessarily having to spell it out.

For example, in 2000, the military Ombudsman's office received complaints regarding the conduct of an internal military investigation of an army training exercise in the early 1990s, which cost the life of a soldier. One of the complainants was related to the deceased and alleged a cover-up of the incident by the military. The other complainant, a senior military leader, was fingered by military investigators as ultimately responsible for the death. He complained of being tagged the fall guy in the case and a scapegoat for the military.[3]

Being an office of last resort, the military Ombudsman suggested to the Army chain of command that serious questions had been raised concerning the conduct of a military board of inquiry, which deserved closer scrutiny. The Army initially agreed to conduct a review of the original investigation at the insistence of the Ombudsman's office. After this commitment and despite several further undertakings, the case was allowed to languish unattended for many months. Faced with the reality that the undertakings by the Army were not about to be fulfilled, the Ombudsman wrote to the head of the Army to inform him that the Ombudsman's office would be proceeding with an investigation of the complaints. Suddenly, the Army announced the beginning of its probe.

Ultimately, the Army grudgingly accepted the commitment to begin its investigation when it realized that the Ombudsman had given up waiting and was going to proceed with his own investigation. The Army's investigation recently concluded that serious errors were committed during the board of inquiry and it agreed to make amends to both complainants.

Clearly, the Army recognized the injustices after concluding its own investigation of the impugned incident. *But for* the involvement of the Ombudsman, however, both complaints would have been destined to gather dust forever.

How does one demonstrate value in these *but for* cases? On the one hand, it is important not to let these cases slip through the system without the ombudsman claiming due credit for having been a key to their resolution. On the other hand, it is equally important to guard against unwelcome claims that do not acknowledge and credit the organization for their actions.

The best approach in *but for* cases is to document the chronology and narrative of the case publication carefully and accurately in the annual report. In so doing, the ombudsman can still reap the benefits of being the triggering event for the organization's positive action, while the recitation of the narrative keeps the matter in perspective and properly credits the goodwill of others in resolving the matter. Your reporting will also come across as fair and balanced as you highlight not just the negative, but also some of the positive steps being taken by the organization.

"Cause and Effect" Cases

The majority of cases resolved favourably fit in the *cause and effect* category. These are cases where the complainant comes to the ombudsman's office seeking its involvement in the resolution of a case. The ombudsman, through shuttle diplomacy or formal reporting, investigates and recommends the resolution of the matter. The organization then accepts and implements, in total or in part, the proposed settlement. These kinds of cases are distinguished from the *but for* cases in that there is no question that the case was resolved at the behest and through the intervention of the ombudsman.

How then can the ombudsman use *cause and effect* cases to demonstrate value? The approach will, to some degree, depend on whether the matter resolved was a case involving an individual issue or a systemic one. The value checklists detailed below provide questions that may assist in determining if your contribution can demonstrate value beyond assisting in resolving the complaints that come to your office. The points made apply to both individual and systemic issues but have been broken down under the category of cases where they are likely to be the most relevant. The lists are not meant to be exhaustive, but rather illustrative of broader value issues that should be considered when you assess the value of your contribution.

a) Individual Issues

Out of the thousands of cases investigated by ombudsmen, cases deciding individual issues normally far outnumber systemic cases. Individual cases are ones where complainants turn to the office of the ombudsman with problems that are personal to them, but not necessarily rampant in the organization.

In the case of the military Ombudsman, individual issues include abuse of authority, harassment or bullying, disputes over claims and benefits, posting issues, and equipment issues. Regardless of the kind of ombudsman's office or the breadth of the enabling mandate, the one common denominator to individual cases is that the complaint revolves around unfair treatment of an individual.

A word of caution is necessary at the outset. The value of the ombudsman's office in resolving individual issues is very much relative and can easily backfire if the contribution of the office in individual cases is strictly contrasted to the cost of running the office. For example, assume your office can settle one thousand individual issues with a budget of two million dollars. Honouring the cumulative claims of all complainants could cost the organization less than it costs to run your office!

The best demonstration of value will be when you can add up both the value in the resolution of individual and systemic issues, while looking beyond the meaning of value in strict terms.

Any positive resolution of a case is a demonstration of value. It is not necessary to state that when your intervention results in someone obtaining a benefit, monetary or not, you have demonstrated some value. What is most interesting, however, is the more subtle argument that the benefit provided by the ombudsman extends far beyond the immediate, tangible deliverables. There are key points you can make that go far beyond the narrow settlement of a complaint and ensure that you are not selling yourself short in marketing your achievements. The following checklists cover some of the most convincing ones.

i) Value checklist

(1) *Did you resolve a case that no one was able to resolve internally?*

Some cases that come to the ombudsman have been tainted by months, even years, of acrimony arising out of the dispute between the complainant and the organization. Suspicion and distrust by both parties may well have obscured their objectivity and prevented a constructive resolution of the conflict. In some cases, through the years of festering, the complaint may have multiplied into several complaints. The workplace may have become dysfunctional.

For example, the *Poulin* case would, in normal circumstances, have consisted of a simple allegation of abuse of authority against a small group of supervisors.[4] Had it been dealt with expeditiously by the military chain of command when the complaint was originally made, it might have been resolved informally and inexpensively. The inability of the military to investigate promptly and give closure to the matter resulted in both sides of the conflict becoming further embroiled. The complaint grew, seemingly, by the day.

The *Poulin* complaint was eventually referred by the chain of command, with agreement by the complainant, to the Ombudsman's office for investigation. The complainant's mistrust in the chain of command ran so deep that he refused to participate in any investigation that was not conducted by either the Ombudsman's office or a panel that included members of the local media. By the time the complaint reached the Ombudsman's office, it consisted of four volumes of documentation, comprising ninety-five allegations against twenty-four individuals, including senior leaders reaching up to the Chief of the Defence Staff (the head of Canada's military). The Ombudsman's final report was 250 pages long, took twenty-two months to complete, and included more than 100 interviews of eighty-five witnesses across Canada and abroad. It required the review of more than 2,000 pages of interview transcripts and thousands of pages of records. Nonetheless, the military Ombudsman was able to demonstrate his office's value by giving closure to a complaint that had overwhelmed the chain of command. Many recommendations were made and most were accepted. In fact, in an unprecedented move, the Chief of the Defence Staff at that time issued a formal written apology to the complainant, as a result of a recommendation in the final report.

In another case involving alleged harassment and discrimination in a cadet unit, the complainant, who was the father of one of the affected cadets, had become an increasingly painful thorn in the side of cadet authorities. The chain of command's inability to satisfy his increasingly fervent demands had led him to travel from his home in British Columbia across the country to Ottawa, in order to confront the Vice Chief of the Defence Staff (who is in charge of all military cadet units) face-to-face in his office. He had also, through what must have been some diligent effort on his part, obtained the military leader's telephone number at home and had taken to calling him to express his disappointment with the cadet movement and its treatment of his daughter. The Vice Chief of the Defence Staff finally called upon the Ombudsman's office in the hope that an independent investigation might resolve what had escalated into a fairly acrimonious conflict.[5]

The Ombudsman's investigation made a number of recommendations to improve the resolution of conflicts between parents of cadets and the military. The Vice Chief of the Defence Staff, who has since retired, took the time to personally write the Ombudsman to thank him for taking on the challenge of the situation. His successor also acknowledged the office's work stating:

Your efforts have ensured the matter was thoroughly reviewed and adequately considered in view of a difficult but significant complaint, which had not been adequately resolved until now. There are many good points in this report and the program will benefit from the fact that all stakeholders will have the ability to use this information in order to further improve the Canadian Cadet movement.[6]

In other instances, internal investigations may have been tainted by "tunnel vision" and spin, fuelled by the need to reach exculpatory conclusions instead of objective and impartial findings. Such "investigations", far from being fact-finding processes, often inflame complainants and make matters worse. The ombudsman can demonstrate his value by providing the necessary neutral thorough gathering and analysis of the facts. For example, in expressing his gratitude for a recent high profile investigation conducted by the military Ombudsman, who concluded that an Army-sanctioned event humiliated a group of injured soldiers, the head of the Army wrote that a prior internal investigation of the same issues by the Army "lacked the rigor and depth needed to uncover the facts. You were able to expose the roots of disrespect held by some [...] We value the role that your office brought to this investigation and appreciate the insight you have provided us to address our shortcomings in this case".[7]

(2) Did you provide an alternative avenue to a more expensive dispute resolution mechanism?

Saving precious resources is always a very compelling way to demonstrate your value.[8] In 2002-2003, the military Ombudsman has conducted three major investigations dealing with how the military treats its members suffering from operational stress injuries, including post traumatic stress disorder (PTSD). The investigations spanned both individual and systemic issues.

The first report, titled *Special Report: Systemic Treatment of CF Members with PTSD,*[9] made what were considered at the time far-reaching recommendations. It warned that failure to promptly address the plight of psychologically injured soldiers could lead them to take the matter into their own hands and sue the government, perhaps resulting in a class action lawsuit. The report stated that there were significant financial implications of failure to deal appropriately with PTSD in the Canadian Forces: by not providing its members with appropriate care, the military might be laying itself open to litigation. In the United Kingdom, the courts had awarded considerable sums to soldiers who were not suitably treated when they were diagnosed with PTSD. In one case, a soldier who served in the Falkland Islands was awarded £100,000 (US $159,000) after the High Court found that the army had failed to treat his PTSD. The military Ombudsman also referred to media reports that over 300 veterans were suing the UK Ministry of Defence for its alleged failure to diagnose and treat PTSD, for a potential cost of £15 million (US $24 million).[10]

Although the High Court in London recently dismissed allegations that the Ministry of Defence had systematically failed to protect service personnel from the psychological consequences of their exposure to the horrors of war, updated numbers estimated that the legal action ended up costing taxpayers a staggering £9 million (US $14 million).[11] In addition, new published accounts of the case estimated that the Ministry of Defence's legal exposure had been closer to £100 million (US $159 million), for a total potential cost of £109 million (US $173 million).[12]

Number-crunching the potential ramifications of not acting to fix problems with the military's treatment of its injured soldiers underlined the value of the office in indicating risks to which the organization was exposed; it also had a strong persuasive effect on senior leadership to act. Out of the thirty-one recommendations that were made in the Ombudsman's report, thirty were accepted and acceptance of the last recommendation is pending.

(3) Will the implementation of the recommended course of action save the organization money?

In his *PTSD* report, the military Ombudsman pointed out that the financial costs of reforming the treating practices of military members with PTSD were insignificant when compared with the costs of recruiting and training a replacement.[13] In addition, the Canadian military's ranks were depleted to the tune of thousands due to members leaving because of PTSD. The Ombudsman established that the minimum cost of developing a basic infantry soldier to the point where he or she is considered combat-ready and experienced is approximately US $226,000. The cost to the institution of losing thousands of trained and experienced soldiers was therefore staggering. Shortly after the release of the report, the military acknowledged that the cost of implementing the recommendations, which would go a long way to fixing the issues raised, was minimal.

(4) Did your intervention settle a relatively inexpensive dispute that was causing a negative ripple effect on morale in the organization?

Sometimes, relatively small individual disputes "hit a raw nerve" with a specific group of stakeholders and spread like wildfire. For example, it may be that the organization follows the rules too rigidly and does not allow for common sense to prevail. In other instances, a lack of proper risk management of conflicts leads to bureaucratic decisions that do not allow for the flexibility needed to properly settle individual problems.

In its 2001-2002 annual report, the military Ombudsman's office signalled a disturbing trend in its caseload by shining the spotlight on a failure of leadership that was causing morale problems among the troops.[14] The message was that military leaders were failing to consider the needs of the "little guy" in making decisions affecting the welfare of troops. In the news release announcing the publication of the annual report, the office pointed out, in demonstrating the value of its services, that members "had become so disheartened by their struggle with the organization that they wanted to leave the forces—until the Ombudsman's office intervened to resolve their problem".[15]

A recent case shows that the military still has ways to go in making administrative decisions that take into consideration the impact on individuals under their command. In *Richmond,* ten junior military members were sent on a 102-day course far away from their homes. Before they went, they were told by the Canadian Forces that they would be entitled to $50 a day to cover meals and other expenses and given cash advances to cover the costs. Some used the money to provide child-care in their absence, which ultimately allowed them to participate. On their return home, they were advised by the bureaucracy at National Defence Headquarters that they had been given the wrong information and that they owed the Canadian Forces approximately $3,000 each—a very significant sum for corporals and master corporals. One even had to sell his house to pay back the money. In appealing to headquarters to reconsider the clawback, complainants were advised by e-mail, in rather callous language that: "The bottom line is that DND is not a benefits smorgasbord and if military members decide to be treated as civilians, then there are options available".[16]

The issues raised in the case traveled quickly through all levels of the organization as an example of coldhearted bureaucratic decision-making. Morale plummeted and, unsurprisingly, there were few volunteers for the next course.

Interestingly, the member's immediate superiors attempted to intervene on their behalf—without success. Adding fuel to the fire, the department that had run the course admitted that its staff were the ones who had erred by giving inaccurate information, but that they had set aside the money and were willing to absorb the cost. Everyone, including the bureaucracy, acknowledged that the members were in no way responsible for the position they were in. Regardless, the Department of National Defence insisted that the money be paid back.

The members filed a number of internal grievances—all of which required a significant amount of the organization's time and resources to process. In fact, it has been estimated that grievances that go through a certain route within the organization average $100,000 each to process.[17] These grievances had yet to be resolved some fifteen months after the course ended. While normally the military Ombudsman will not look at an incident while it is being dealt with by existing mechanisms, in this case, he decided to intervene because of the compelling circumstances—the immediate and serious financial impact on the involved members. His staff initially attempted to resolve the issue informally with the bureaucracy, but was unable to reach an agreement that the Ombudsman deemed fair.

Ultimately, the military Ombudsman's office conducted a full investigation and made recommendations to the general in charge of personnel. The main recommendation—you may not be surprised to hear—was that the affected members not be forced to pay back the money. A preliminary response from headquarters thanked the Ombudsman for his "extensive" analysis of the case and promised to explore resolution options.

Cases such as these, which illustrate iron-fist decision-making, are a lighting rod for serious morale problems and, as a result, reduce the productivity of the organization. The ombudsman can demonstrate the value of his office and contribute to good morale by helping to inject common sense into decision-making and by encouraging managers to adopt best practices.

(5) Do you produce sound data on trends in cases coming to your office?

Just as "a picture is worth a thousand words", presenting a picture of the total number of cases in which you helped individuals in need will speak volumes about the value you bring to your stakeholders.

The military Ombudsman's annual report contains summaries of the types of complaints received, their origin and the results obtained, including the number of investigations, substantiated complaints, unsubstantiated complaints, and successful resolutions. The Ombudsman's office also sends quarterly statistical updates to senior managers and military leaders, which invariably leads to requests throughout the year for further information on types of complaints and trends arising within different units and geographic areas. For example, a change in command recently occurred for the Army in the province of Quebec. The new commander wished to start off on the right foot and wanted to make a concerted effort to deal with issues of concern to the rank and file under his command and their families. In order to make sure he truly had his finger on the pulse of the troops, he requested that the Ombudsman's office provide him with some insights through a statistical breakdown of the types of complaints the office received from his area, as well as a meeting with the Ombudsman himself to discuss trends and specific issues of concern.

It is important to keep in mind that it is not just the numbers themselves that are important, but also what sense you can make of them. Trends in increases and decreases of certain types of complaints, geographical distributions, and information on who is bringing complaints forward are of considerable value to the organization. This information allows leaders to keep in touch with the issues of concern to their members or employees and to measure whether or not they are being responsive to them. Ombudsman analysis of trends in complaints can be an important measure of whether institutional responses to a specific problem have been effective. For example, when the military Ombudsman's office was created, the Canadian military was facing continual scandal over incidents of sexual assault and sexual harassment. The Ombudsman's office received an influx of complaints in 1998 and 1999, even before it officially opened its doors for business. This issue was so significant and pressing at the time that the Ombudsman chose a case involving systemic issues related to the treatment of sexual assault victims in the military to be the subject of the office's first public report.[18] After five years of operations, the Ombudsman was able to report that, following a number of strong messages from the military chain of command and concerted military and federal government initiatives to combat harassment, the number of complaints received about sexual assault, sexual harassment, and the treatment of victims has decreased from 1998's rather discouraging figures.

The independent information and statistics produced by the ombudsman on the types of complaints received and trends in the organization can also provide valuable guidance to steer future change. For example, an independent legislative reviewer was appointed recently to evaluate changes that were implemented to Canada's *National Defence Act* in the area of military justice and to put forward recommendations for future reforms. The Minister of National Defence included in the reviewer's terms of reference that he consult with the Ombudsman's office as an independent source of information on trends in military justice issues. The office quickly became an invaluable source of information to the reviewer on trends in complaints coming from military members related to the military justice system. These complaints include breakdowns in the system designed to handle internal military grievances and concerns of conflict of interest, which have arisen as the result of the military lawyers under the command of the Judge Advocate General assuming responsibility for the adjudication of grievances.

(6) Did your investigation discover a cover-up of the truth or other ethical lapse?

At any time in history, cover-ups and ethical lapses are symptoms of trouble. In this post-Enron, post-Worldcom era, the sensitivity regarding ethical issues is further heightened. Private and public institutions are expected to be transparent and conduct themselves fairly. The ombudsman who can detect instances of bad ethical behaviour or decision-making will prove valuable to stakeholders.

In one of the first major investigations of the military Ombudsman in 1999, the office reported on its conclusions in a case involving allegations of conflict of interest. In the *Smith* case, the Ombudsman's office upheld a complaint that a military police officer was investigating a suspect with whom he had been closely involved both professionally and personally.[19] Until the final report was made public, the head of the military police vehemently denied any notion of conflict, in part because the military police officer was not listed in the organizational chart pertaining to the ongoing investigation. Yet, the evidence provided by the military police itself showed the officer was not hermetically sealed from the case. He continued to attend investigative meetings where the *Smith* case was discussed and strategic decisions were made. In addition, the organizational chart produced by the military police demonstrated that investigators reporting to the military police officer in question were tasked with working directly on the *Smith* case.

Despite the clear ethical issue of conflict of interest, the outside eye of the military Ombudsman and his publicly reported findings were needed to convince authorities to remove the military police officer from the case.

More recently, in March 2003, the military Ombudsman released the *Crazy Train* report, stemming from an incident best described as a take on the movie *Animal House*.[20] On a military base, under orders from the commander, infantry soldiers constructed a float depicting a train pulling a cage. Inside the cage was a young male soldier dressed provocatively in women's clothing. The cage bore signs that revealed to those with local knowledge that the float was meant to lampoon members with operational stress injuries. Alcohol abuse was reportedly rampant during the incident. Four hundred soldiers were present, including women. A large number of the male soldiers were dressed up in women's clothing.

One aspect of the military Ombudsman's investigation into this incident was whether or not the military's original internal investigation was adequate. The Ombudsman concluded that it was not. The report qualified the military's investigation of the matter as a "pseudo-investigation" that, instead of being thorough and objective, consisted of cursory inquiries designed to put the issues "to bed". The report's final comment was that "a real investigation would have uncovered the truth".[21]

In response to the *Crazy Train* report, the Chief of the Defence Staff wrote to the Ombudsman that he found the events detailed by the office "disturbing" and, in dealing with the substantive complaint, commented that "the inherent lack of sensitivity—to ethnic, gender, and especially mental health issues—in evidence is truly "worrisome".[22] Furthermore, he requested that the head of the Army report back to him why his chain of command "could not recognize or address [the seriousness of the incident] without resort to external investigation".[23]

In both the *Smith* and *Crazy Train* cases, the military Ombudsman demonstrated value by uncovering ethical problems the organization had been unable or unwilling to discover on its own.

(7) Did your investigation of a specific complaint shed light on a related matter that was not the subject of a complaint?

If, indeed, as stated in *The American Heritage Dictionary of the English Language,* a Pandora's box is "a source of many unforeseen troubles",[24] then the ombudsman can be accused at times of opening a Pandora's box. Nevertheless, in doing so, the ombudsman will have shown value to the organization by allowing it to discover its problems before they mushroom into much larger ones. In the *Crazy Train* report, for example, while investigating the allegations that an infantry unit had mocked victims with operational stress injuries, Ombudsman investigators uncovered undeveloped official photographs of the parade taken by the military base's photographer. One of the photographs, reproduced in the published report, depicted a soldier dressed up in woman's clothing, complete with a thong.[25] One of the unpublished photographs depicted a male soldier with full genital exposure. The investigation also related how some witnesses had stated that alcohol was a factor in the incident. Although the Ombudsman's investigation was limited to the issue in the complaint, the mocking of operational stress injury among soldiers, the Chief of the Defence Staff's response to the report extended far beyond the Ombudsman's findings. He not only accepted these findings and the Ombudsman's recommendation, but also ordered a further probe of related issues, such as gender.

The greatest vehicle to demonstrate your value in treating individual issues is to publicize the results of your intervention. Needless to say, the publication of the case should be tasteful and respectful of the confidentiality expectations of the complainant. In the *Crazy Train* case, the military Ombudsman decided to include one of the photographs of the incident, which graphically illustrated the Pandora's box of issues his investigation brought to light.[26]

b) Systemic Issues

A systemic issue is one that relates to the administrative processes or practices in an organization and affects more than one person in an organization. A systemic problem may be a flaw in an approach or line of thinking or it may be rooted in that organization's very culture.

Systemic investigations can prove to be very expensive endeavours. Done right, they involve intense research and analysis, but they can yield very high dividends to the ombudsman in demonstrating his value. When fixing a systemic problem, dozens, hundreds, or even thousands of individuals may benefit.

i) Value checklist

(1) Did your office discover a cultural problem that caused deep malaise within a stakeholder group?

One of the clear advantages of an arms-length investigator, such as an ombudsman, looking into issues affecting an organization is that he brings to the table fresh, objective, and impartial eyes to study a situation. Human nature and pride in one's work sometimes lead organizations not only to be blind to a problem, but also to go into denial over its very existence. Not being able to acknowledge a problem prevents it from being fixed.

When looking at cultural issues, the situation is exacerbated by the fact the organization is often intertwined with the individuals who are part of it, leading them to be blind to the obvious. The more insular the organization, the more likely this will happen. A military organization that relies on hierarchy and obeying orders is perhaps the most fertile ground for breeding this approach. Nothing illustrates this point better than the *Crazy Train* episode.

Despite behaviour that should have been loudly denounced by members, the military Ombudsman received only one complaint. When it became known that one of the soldiers had complained, the office received reports that efforts were being made to weed out who had brought disrepute on the unit for complaining.

While the attitudes displayed in the *Crazy Train* episode were no doubt based more on ignorance than malice, they were deep-seated and long-standing. The Ombudsman's demonstration of value was to censure the kind of culture that allowed this incident to occur, by highlighting how blatant and unabashed the culture of inappropriate and destructive attitudes about operational stress injuries is.

The Chief of the Defence Staff commented in a letter to the Ombudsman that he "would have expected that we were beyond the potential for this sort of cultural manifestation".[27] The head of the Army added his voice to the issue by writing the following:

> In light of your findings and recommendations [...] I will be undertaking a full review of all cultural related activities (including OSI [operational stress injuries]) within the army, to assess the progress we are making, in order that current programmes be shaped to better achieve our objectives.[28]

Both leaders recognized that the Ombudsman's discovery of cultural problems within the Canadian military, which were denounced once they became widely known, was a contribution of value to the organization.

(2) Did your investigation contribute to or echo corporate priorities?

It is trite to say that the *raison d'être* of an ombudsman's investigation is not to advance corporate priorities, which may be part of a broader systemic problem. The ombudsman must, at all times, be concerned with issues of fairness.

However, in reaching findings in a given case, the ombudsman's conclusions in a systemic case may well complement corporate objectives and priorities. For example, the ombudsman should draw on the "people" themes that often drive corporate business plans and priorities that correspond with the objectives of ombudsman work. Government and private sector enterprises illustrate the "people" themes by adopting expression along the lines of "our strength is people" or "people are our most valued asset".

The Canadian Chief of the Defence Staff's webpage on corporate priorities lists "putting people first" as the top priority.[29] In his response to the Ombudsman's *Crazy Train* report, the Chief of the Defence Staff did not miss the opportunity to thank the office for contributing value to the organization by pointing out an incident that showed that the military leadership needed to be reminded of the "putting people first" philosophy.[30] He wrote that the cultural manifestations are "clearly [...] not the sort of activities appropriate to a progressive institution of choice that professes to 'putting people first'".[31] The Chief added that he had tasked the human resources branch of the military to set up a mental health awareness program to "reinforce a positive attitude and supportive ethos across the Canadian Forces."[32]

"While recognizing the importance of tradition and custom in the maintenance of esprit de corps," he stated, "such traditions must reflect our institutional values and standards. I cannot endorse in any way this type of behaviour from CF personnel. The enculturation of CF members in general, and of the Army in particular, is expected to be of the highest societal order".[33] The head of the Army's response reinforced the Chief of the Defence Staff's position and vowed to continue working to better educate soldiers about operational stress injuries.

If applicable, the military Ombudsman's office emphasizes to the military leadership how a particular recommendation contributes to the realization of corporate goals. Thus, in creating the right linkages between the recommendations you make and the corporate priorities of the organization, you are demonstrating your value by reinforcing a corporate message to senior managers.

(3) Do the organization's field practices contradict head office's prescriptions?

Large organizations like to create guidelines and rules emanating from head office. Some of these prescriptions are ambiguous "feel good" directives that are hard to define, such as "everyone shall treat an employee/customer with dignity and respect". However, some of these directives may be measurable and worded more as employee/customer entitlements instead of "wish lists".

Your investigation may uncover that an injustice has occurred because the directives from head office were ignored by sub-offices, which found them too labour intensive or inconvenient. You will have demonstrated your value by illustrating the contradictions between theory and practice and by recommending how to fill the gap. For example, in his follow-up report on PTSD, the military Ombudsman informed stakeholders about the military's response to his original *PTSD* report and the efforts made to implement the theity-one recommendations it contained.[34] The Ombudsman was able to report that there was a renewed sense of determination at senior levels in the organization to move the issues forward. Tangible progress was evident. He noted, however, that there was a significant "disconnect" at the unit level in implementing important initiatives such as outreach training, which were required to change the culture of stigma and ostracism faced by those who suffer from PTSD. Although the direction to implement training programs was coming down from National Defence Headquarters and money was being made available to treatment centres to provide training, many units were not requesting it.

In describing this disconnect between senior management's commitments and the actions of those in the field, the Ombudsman noted:

> In my opinion the situation is somewhat analogous to the heart (the strong support of senior management) pumping, but the major problems with the blood getting to the extremities (the culture in the field) where it is needed. In this case, the clogged arteries that are causing the slowdowns and blockages are lined with bureaucracy. The longer it takes to clear the arteries and start some of these improvements, the more difficult it will be to deal with the entrenched problems.[35]

The Outreach Tools

Conducting fair and objective investigations highlighting how you are adding value to stakeholders will only achieve its purpose if they are combined with effective outreach. Your goal is to disseminate your value in such a way as to have maximum positive impact.

Using outreach as a means of demonstrating your value by showcasing the strides your office has made is a delicate proposition. You want and need to illustrate to stakeholders that you can make a difference in their lives. If you deprive yourself of this ability, you will be severely limiting yourself to demonstrating value only to the complainant. On the other hand, outreach, particularly involving the media, needs to be done judiciously or you risk over-exposing yourself and being branded as someone with an agenda. Note that even a judicious approach executed with the greatest amount of care and planning will not always convince the sceptics of your good intentions.

A well-organized, competent communications support unit is one of the most important functions in an ombudsman's office. The unit will ensure that the message is not only well packaged, but delivered at a time and place to maximize the intended result.

What are the outreach tools?

There are basically two kinds of communications tools you can use to demonstrate your value. You can create a product that conveys the value message or you can communicate the message verbally through meetings, interviews, and other face-to-face situations. Depending on the job you want done, you will use a different tool or a different set of tools. Using them in combination can help reinforce the message. For example, the military Ombudsman often produces a

118

report calling for policy change, holds a press conference to announce its release and simultaneously makes it available on his website.

a) Products

The list of products you can use to demonstrate your value is virtually endless. It includes annual reports, brochures, newsletters, websites, multimedia products, and promotional items.

b) Face-to-face

There are many ways to convey your message to stakeholders. You may choose to use the media by conducting one-on-one interviews, calling press conferences, or meeting with editorial boards of newspapers. Alternately, you can speak directly to your key stakeholders at town hall meetings, award ceremonies and other events hosted or attended by key stakeholders.

How to Wield Them

In order to "hit the nail on the head", you need to know what you are aiming at. Who is your target audience? What do they want to hear? What do they *need* to hear? How do they need to hear it? Keeping the target in mind, use the following tips to really make the product and face-to-face tools work for you.

a) Audience Appeal

i) Be responsive

In this age of information overload, if your product, event, or message does not appeal to your audience, it will not have much impact. The message must be tailor-made for the audience and responsive to its needs.

For example, when the office of the military Ombudsman was created in June 1998, it was the focus of much publicity given the fact that it was created in response to high profile military scandals involving abuse of authority. The publicity led to a large influx of new cases arriving with the announcement of its creation. Unfortunately, the Ombudsman's mandate was provided one year later. There was much interest among stakeholders at that time as to the number of cases backlogged and how the office would tackle this and other challenges.

As an early demonstration of value to stakeholders, the office committed to publishing a one hundred day report detailing the kinds of cases received by the office and their status (active or resolved). Furthermore, much publicity surrounding the office in its first year had focused on the "pockets of resistance" within the ranks of senior military leaders, which, at the time, appeared to stand firm in their opposition to civilian oversight. The *100 Day Report Card* gave an opportunity for the military Ombudsman to reach out to senior leadership in an attempt to diffuse the resistance to his office.[36]

ii) Be accessible

Large corporations and governments publish reports that are not always the simplest to understand. Similarly, speeches and presentations featuring unintelligible exploding pie charts are relied on all too frequently in social clubs and conferences to illustrate a point. Readers respond by not reading such reports. Listeners respond by tuning out. Whatever outreach strategy is employed, verbal or written, the use of simple straightforward language will make your message much more likely to be absorbed than elaborate prose or pretentious pie charts.

iii) Be creative and (a bit) daring

Annual reports are the most frequent means by which ombudsmen communicate with stakeholders and account for the value of their activities. The reports should be carefully crafted for their main audience. The military Ombudsman's annual reports have raised a few eyebrows through the years, but they have also garnered much praise for their creativity and innovation. The controversy surrounding the military Ombudsman's annual reports concerns the use of light spirited language and illustrations to complement the narrative of cases resolved informally.

Every year, the office handles approximately 2,000 cases and features about twenty case synopses in its annual report. These illustrate the kinds of cases the office has resolved and demonstrates the value of its interventions. The military Ombudsman's office considers this a unique opportunity to showcase its value to its clientele, which is generally comprised of non-commissioned soldiers, sailors, and air personnel who, at the best of times, are deluged with reports and paperwork of all kinds. In order to stand out from the pile of documents and be read by this important stakeholder group, the annual reports adopt a lighter humorous tone. From the feedback the office receives every year, this has proven to be very successful with all but a few senior leaders who have expressed concern that the Ombudsman's reports are not consistent with the "look and feel" of the military.

The 2002-2003 annual report, for example, describes how the military Ombudsman's intervention helped get rid of bats that had taken hold of a soldier and his family's quarters on a base. The following story appeared in the annual report along with a descriptive cartoon:

120

It's Driving Us Batty!

These CF members, though usually quite fond of animals, found living with a slew of unwanted flying rodents less than appealing.

They visited the office in the summer regarding a 'pest' problem they were having in their Private Married Quarters (PMQ). It seems they had some housemates in the form of bats. These bats took house in the attic, but managed to leave their droppings all over the PMQ. The members had tried to resolve their problem with the Canadian Forces Housing Agency (CFHA), but to no avail.

The investigator assigned to the case contacted the CFHA, and was successful in getting someone to the PMQ to remove the bats, and prevent them from coming in again - or so it seemed.

Despite these measures, the persistent bats found another way into the quarters. The investigator called the CFHA again to report that the pest problem had in fact not been resolved. This time, the CFHA sent over both their Chief Inspector and a contractor to finally put an end to the issue. The result? The bats were banished from the PMQ with no way back in, much to the members' satisfaction.[37]

iv) Focus on the human interest angle

These stories also work the human interest angle, widely used by the media as a way to appeal to their audience. Because ombudsmen are in the business of helping people, they often have good human interest stories to tell. When crafting a product or talking to stakeholders, make it clear how the issues you are raising affect real people. The military ombudsman ensures his reports are compelling by including relevant snippets from interviews conducted during an investigation. For example, the *PTSD* report described how the macho military culture affects soldiers suffering from stress injuries. Quotes from soldiers are peppered throughout the analysis, to illustrate the problem in the words of the people affected. For example: "It is like running with a wolf pack. It's fine when you are running with the pack. The minute you start bleeding or limping then they you are on you."[38] Through quotes from real people, the urgency and seriousness of the issue that prompted the investigation come through in the final report and help push decision-makers to action.

v) Hit close to home

If the resolution of a problem has a far greater interest locally than nationally, focus on the local ways to get your message out. In the *Crazy Train* case mentioned previously, the military Ombudsman held a press conference to communicate his investigation's results in the same city as the military base where the incident occurred. The local media coverage was intense and the story also got picked up across Canada. The local military chain of command followed with their own press conference at the same location, in which they endorsed the acceptance of the Ombudsman's recommendations by the Chief of the Defence Staff.

vi) It's all about timing

Choosing *when* to use your communications tools is just as important as choosing *which* tool to use. Consider what is going on in your audience's environment—certain times will likely stand out as better than others. In some cases, synergy with other events can help generate interest for your cause. For example, the public release of a report on the management of a treatment centre for soldiers suffering from operational stress injuries was timed to coincide with the release of the results of a survey measuring the incidence of mental health issues, including operational stress injuries, among soldiers.

Other people's deadlines may also affect your choice of timing. The military Ombudsman makes a point of releasing his annual report before Parliament rises for summer holidays, since experience has shown that interest in political issues tends to wane once the parliamentary debates are over. Knowing how the media operate is also important. In Canada's capital city, holding a press conference late Friday afternoon is almost guaranteed to bury your message.

vii) Align your message with audience values

Demonstrating a link between your recommendation and a value your audience holds dear is a good way to encourage buy-in. When speaking to stakeholders about his recommendations to improve the treatment of soldiers with stress injuries, the military Ombudsman referred to the time-honoured military ethic that leaders have a responsibility to take care of their troops. He also highlighted how those who fall victim to the disorder are often the best and most dedicated soldiers. In another case dealing with unfair clawbacks, the Ombudsman's recommendations were couched in terms of "a promise is a promise". In a similar case involving an administrative foul up, the Ombudsman cited a message that had previously been sent by the Chief of the Defence Staff to commanders, stating that soldiers should not have to bear the burden when an error is made or bad advice received.

b) Learn the Tricks of the Media Trade

Using the media can be an invaluable but sometimes risky way of demonstrating your value. However, when you know how to do it right, the dividends are enormous. If speaking to the media forms a significant part of demonstrating your value, it is probably worth investing in training with a reputable media trainer. You will learn the tricks of the trade and get the chance to practice answering the hard questions before you go live.

c) Strike a Balance

Sometimes marketing your value can come into conflict with other key aspects of your work. Striking the right balance is critical to your organization's credibility and public profile. Communicating your office's results, a critical part of demonstrating your value, can sometimes come into conflict with your responsibility to maintain complainant confidentiality. You may find yourself making judgment calls about whether writing a human-interest story about one of your cases would reveal too much about a particular complainant. Would reaching out to your stakeholders through your organization's newsletter have a negative impact on your independence? There is no easy answer to these questions. However, by finding the right balance, you will be emphasizing the value of the core tenets upon which you base your practice.

d) Remember the Three Cs

The bottom line is that to be effective, all communications efforts should be:

Clear: It is difficult to convince someone of something if they are not sure what you are saying. Keep in mind that if you have worked extensively on an issue, things that seem obvious to you may not be clear to others. It is often useful to bounce drafts off someone who was not intimately involved with the project. They can help you identify confusing language or logical leaps.

Concise: Too many details will dilute your message. Decide what is necessary for your specific audience, then chop the rest. This will help your audience retain what is important.

Correct: Needless to say, your credibility hinges on the correctness of your information. Check your facts, then check them again. If a mistake does happen, honesty is the best policy. Admit it, apologize, then get back on track with the right information.

Conclusion

In conclusion, the most important thing for ensuring your success is monitoring your effectiveness at demonstrating your value. All your effort in planning, strategizing, and finally sending the right messages to your stakeholders will be futile if th[18]e message is not received. For every report the military Ombudsman releases, the office evaluates the media coverage it received in terms of audience reach or advertising value, monitors the number of hits on the office's website, and records feedback received through the office's toll free intake line.

In 2003, with the simultaneous launch of the military Ombudsman's annual report and environmental exposure investigation,[19] the media coverage figures were most impressive. The annual report and the environmental exposure investigation were covered by 17 daily newspapers, 21 different radio stations, and 14 different television stations all across Canada. Using circulation and audience averages, the total potential audience was approximately seven million people, almost a quarter of the Canadian public. These figures, along with the e-mails and letters of support from internal and external stakeholders and the number of submissions for the environmental exposure investigation, indicate that indeed the message has been well received and the value of the office, it is hoped, well demonstrated.

Endnotes

1.   Department of National Defence and the Canadian Forces, *Ministerial Directives*, online: The Ombudsman for the Department of National Defence and the Canadian Forces <http://www.ombudsman.forces.gc.ca/mandate/ministerialDirectives_-e.asp#ombudsman> (date accessed: September 3, 2004) at s. 3((1)(c).

2.   The Ombudsman for the Department of National Defence and the Canadian Forces, *The Way Forward: Action Plan for the Office of the Ombudsman* (January 1999) at 39. Hardcopy available from the Office of the Ombudsman.

3.   The Ombudsman for the Department of National Defence and the Canadian Forces, *When a Soldier Falls: Reviewing the response to MCpl Rick Wheeler's Accidental Death*, online: The Ombudsman for the Department of National Defence and the Canadian Forces <http://www.ombudsman.forces.gc.ca/reports/special/SoldierFalls/contents_e.asp> (dates accessed: February 1, 2005).

4.   The Ombudsman for the Department of National Defence and the Canadian Forces, *Allegations Against the Canadian Forces, Complainant Captain Bruce Poulin*, online: The Ombudsman for the Department of National Defence and the Canadian Forces <http://www.ombudsman.forces.gc.ca/reports/special/Poulin-toc_e.asp> (date accessed: September 3, 2004).

5.   Letter from the Vice Chief of the Defence Staff to the miltary Ombudsman (July 12, 2000).

6.   Letter from the Vice Chief of the Defence Staff to the military Ombudsman (February 9, 2002).

7.   Letter from the Chief of the Land Staff to the military Ombudsman (February 28, 2003).

8.   Implementing a recommendation that results in cost savings can also be a very effective way to convince the authorities to accept the recommendation.

9.   The Ombudsman for the Department of National Defence and the Canadian Forces *Systemic Treatment of CF Members with PTSD*, Complainant: Christian McEachern, online: The Ombudsman for the Department of National Defence and the Canadian Forces <http://www.ombudsman.forces.gc.ca/reports/special/PTSD-toc_e.asp> (date accessed: September 3, 2004).

10.   Richard Norton-Taylor "Ex-service personnel to sue over trauma" *The Guardian* (April 3, 2001).

11.   Clare Dyer and Sarah Boseley "War veterans lose trauma claim case" *The Guardian* (May 22, 2003).

12.   *Ibid*.

13.   *Supra* note 9.

14.   The Ombudsman for the Department of National Defence and the Canadian Forces, *Annual Report 2001-2002* (June 2002), online: The Ombudsman for the Department of National Defence and the Canadian Forces <http://www.ombudsman.forces.gc.ca/reports/annual/2001-2002_e.asp? view=graphical> (date accessed: September 3, 2004).

15. The Ombudsman for the Department of National Defence and the Canadian Forces, News release, "Ombudsman Finds Military Decisions Too Often Overlook Soldiers Needs" (June 18, 2002), online: The Ombudsman for the Department of National Defence and the Canadian Forces <http://www.ombudsman.forces.gc.ca/mediaRoom/newsReleases /2002/06-18_e.asp? view=graphical> (date accessed: September 3, 2004).

16. E-mail from officer at National Defence Headquarters to complainants (July 2, 2002).

17. *The First Independent Review by the Right Honourable Antonio Lamer P.C., C.C., C.D. of the provisions and operation of Bill C-25, An Act to amend the National Defence Act and to make consequential amendments to other Acts, as required under section 96 of Statutes of Canada 1998*, c. 35, September 3, 2003. At p. 104. Online: The Ombudsman for the Department of National Defence and the Canadian Forces http://www.dnd.ca/site/Reports/review/en/report_e.pdf> (date accessed: February 16, 2003).

18. The Ombudsman for the Department of National Defence and the Canadian Forces, *Systemic Treatment of Sexual Assault*, Case Reference 99-023 (November 22, 1999). Hardcopy available from the Office of the Ombudsman.

19. The Ombudsman for the Department of National Defence and the Canadian Forces, *Allegation of Conflict of Interest*, Case Reference 99-424, 99-443 (October 20, 1999). Hardcopy available from the Office of the Ombudsman.

20. Special Ombudsman Response Team, *Off the Rails: Crazy Train Float Mocks Operational Stress Injury Sufferers* (March 2003), online: The Ombudsman for the Department of National Defence and the Canadian Forces <http://www.ombudsman.forces.gc.ca/report/special/OTR-01e.asp? view=graphical> (date accessed: September 3, 2004) [*Crazy Train*].

21. *Ibid.*

22. Letter from the Chief of the Defence Staff to the military Ombudsman (February 13, 2003).

23. *Ibid.*

24. *The American Heritage Dictionary of the English Language*, 4th ed., s.v. "Pandora's box".

25. *Supra* note 20 at 12.

26. The photo in the *Crazy Train* report was carefully chosen from among several pictures, some more graphic, to best illustrate the point of the investigation.

27. *Supra* note 22.

28. *Supra* note 7.

29. See e.g. Chief of the Defence Staff, *Corporate Priorities for Defence 2003-2004*, online: Department of National Defence <http://www.cds.forces.gc.ca/pubs/priorities_e.asp> (date assessed: September 3, 2004); The Ombudsman for the Department of National Defence and the Canadian Forces, *Report on Plans and Priorities, 2003*, online: The Ombudsman for the Department of National Defence and the Canadian Forces <http://www.eds.forces.gc.ca/pubs/priorities_e.asp> (date accessed: September 3, 2004).

30. *Supra* note 22.

31. *Ibid.*

32. *Ibid.*

33. *Ibid.*

34. The Ombudsman for the Department of National Defence and the Canadian Forces, *Follow-up Report: Review of DND/CF Actions on Operational Stress Injuries*, online: The Ombudsman for the Department of National Defence and the Canadian Forces, <http://www.forces.gc.ca/reports/special/OSI-toc e.asp>.

35. *Ibid.* at para. 21.

36. The Ombudsman for the Department of National Defence and the Canadian Forces *100 Day Report Card* (September 1999). Hardcopy available from the Office for the Ombudsman.

37.   The Ombudsman for the Department of National Defence and the Canadian Forces, *Annual Report*, 2002-2003, at 30, online: The Ombudsman for the Department of National Defence and the Canadian Forces <http://www.ombudsman.forces.gc.ca /reports/annual /2002 -2003_e.asp-case>.

38.   *Supra* note 9 at para. 501.

39.   The Ombudsman for the Department of National Defence and the Canadian Forces, News Release, "DND/CF Ombudsman Launches New Investigation Into Environmental Exposure" (June 5, 2003), online: The Ombudsman for the Department of National Defence and the Canadian Forces   <http://www.ombudsman.forces.gc.ca /mediaRoom/newsRelease/2003/07-05_e.asp> (date accessed: September 3, 2004).

THE CHARTER OF FUNDAMENTAL RIGHTS OF THE EUROPEAN UNION: A LANDMARK IN THE EUROPEAN LANDSCAPE AND THE PROSPECT FOR A DYNAMIC ROLE OF THE OMBUDSMAN

Catarina Sampaio Ventura & João Zenha Martins[*]

Les institutions européennes ont proclamé, en 2000, la Charte de droits fondamentaux de l'Union européenne. Ce document signifie que l'Union est, dès lors, dotée avec son propre et écrite catalogue des droits fondamentaux. En tant que "proclamation solennelle", la Charte ne s'est pas vue être attribuée, formellement, valeur juridique obligatoire. De ce fait, les auteurs débattent la valeur accrue apportée par la Charte en vue de la protection des droits de l'homme et des libertés fondamentales au sein de l'espace de l'Union, aussi bien que la problématique de son caractère juridique. Acceptant que la Charte intègre déjà l'"acquis communautaire" fondamentale qui marque le procès de l'intégration européenne, les auteurs mettent en relief la fonction paramétrique de la Charte au moment de monitoring les comportements de l'Union et de ses Etats membres. Dans ce contexte-là, il est reconnu le rôle que les Ombudsmen, notamment les Ombudsmen des Etats membres de l'Union et le Médiateur européen, peuvent jouer en mobilisant la Charte dans la défense des citoyens contre illégalités ou injustices des pouvoirs publiques.

****

* Assistants of the Private Office of the Portuguese Ombudsman. The views expressed are strictly personal and do not engage the Portuguese Ombudsman. The authors would like to thank Mrs. Karin Franke for her valuable collaboration in the translation into English of an earliest Portuguese version of the present paper.

En el año 2000, las instituciones europeas proclamaron la Carta Constitucional de los Derechos Fundamentales de la Unión Europea. A partir de ese momento, la Unión contó con su propio catálogo escrito de derechos fundamentales. Como "proclamación solemne", a la Carta Constitucional no se le adjudicó formalmente un carácter vinculante. Por ende, los autores discuten el valor agregado consagrado en dicha Carta, en cuanto a la protección de los derechos humanos y las libertades fundamentales dentro de la Unión, así como también la cuestión de la naturaleza legal de la Carta. Los autores sostienen que la Carta ya es parte del "acquis communautaire" fundamental, del proceso de integración, y ponen énfasis en la función de referencia de la Carta cuando se monitorean las acciones y omisiones de la Unión y de los Estados Miembros. En este contexto, el papel que los ombudsmen puedan desempeñar, en especial el Ombudsman Europeo y los Ombudsmen de los Países Miembros, es de importancia, al apoyarse en las normas de la Carta cuando defienden a las personas contra las ilegalidades e injusticias cometidas por entidades públicas.

Introduction

On December 7, 2000, at the Nice European Council, the European Parliament, the Council and the Commission "solemnly proclaimed" the *Charter of Fundamental Rights of the European Union (Charter)*[1], adopting, *ipsis verbis*, the text drafted by an unprecedented body with unparalleled legitimacy within the framework of European construction—the self-denominated "Convention".[2]

In effect, the *Charter* arose out of a body—the above referred "Convention"—endowed with particular democratic legitimacy. The Convention was composed of members both of national parliaments and of the European Parliament, representatives of the heads of state or government of member states, and a representative of the President of the European Commission. It also included representatives of the European Council (including the European Court of Human Rights) and of the Court of Justice of the European Communities as observers.[3]

From the beginning this option as to the drafting process gave an essential legitimating dimension to the Convention, raising the European Union (EU) within the paradigm of the rule of law. So, as far as the adopted text is to be understood as derived from the exercise of the will of the sovereign peoples of the EU member states, a broadened consensus on the content of the *Charter* becomes more evident.[4]

Furthermore, the developments involved in this rule-making process found a significant reception within the framework of the current revision of the EU Treaties considering that text of the draft Treaty establishing a Constitution for Europe, presented to the Thessaloniki European Council, was prepared within the same Convention-based working method.[5]

The Added Value of the *Charter*

Upon the proclamation of the *Charter*, the Union is now endowed with its own written catalogue of fundamental rights. This catalogue represents a notable milestone regarding the protection of these rights within the EU. Composed of fifty substantive articles, the rights enshrined in the *Charter* are grouped in the following six chapters: "Dignity", "Freedoms", "Equality", "Solidarity", "Citizen's rights," and "Justice". This classification clearly demonstrates the broad scope of the *Charter*. The *Charter* encompasses civil and political rights, as well as economic, social, and cultural rights, recovering a sense of the Universal Declaration of Human Rights' principle of indivisibility.

In fact, the *Charter* brings together civil and political rights consecrated in international instruments, with emphasis on the European Convention for the Protection of Human Rights and Fundamental Freedoms (ECHR) and its five Protocols. Moreover, it codifies social rights which, until then, were spread out in documents like the 1989 *Community Charter of the Fundamental Social Rights of Workers* and the *European Social Charter*. Unlike classical instruments of international law, it does so without admitting reservations. This aspect becomes all the more important with regard to social rights as it is precisely within this realm that less normative homogenization is observed among EU member states.

In addition, beyond comprising the citizenship's rights already inscribed in the founding Treaties—the Treaty on European Union (TUE) and the Treaty Establishing the European Community (EC Treaty)—the *Charter*, as the most up-to-date catalogue of fundamental rights at the international level, also embodies the rights that portray the latest developments in safeguarding the dignity of the human person. These rights are embodied in the bioethics domain,[6] as well as in dimensions concerning the so-called "third generation rights" such as environmental protection[7] and consumer protection.[8]

Many of these rights were already an integral part of the Community legal order (*e.g.* freedom of conscience and religion, respect for private life, right to property). Other rights remained outside the potential field of violation as a result of either an action or omission by Community entities. These additional rights have a substantially innovative character concerning the binding effect on the Community decision-maker, limited by the principle of competence. Examples of these additional rights include the right to marry and to found a family[9] and the rights connected with principles of criminal justice.[10] Considering the present state of delimitation of competences between the EU and the member states, such rights are not enshrined within the material scope of Community law as member states reserve competence within these domains.

It is important to stress that the sense of the *Charter's* proclamation only becomes intelligible if one bears in mind the manner and the extent of fundamental rights' protection within the EU, exclusively in light of the founding Treaties. In effect, according to these Treaties, protection of fundamental rights within the Union is essentially based on:

> a) The legal general compromise of the Union regarding respect for these rights, as provided in Article 6, paragraph 2, of the TEU, according to which "the Union shall respect fundamental rights, as guaranteed by the European Convention for the Protection of Human Rights and Fundamental Freedoms [ECHR] signed in Rome on 4 November 1950 and as they result from the constitutional traditions common to the Member States, as general principles of Community law".[11] This provision formalized the consistent case law of the Court of Justice, which, in the framework of the extant praetorian protection of fundamental rights, already included those rights as a component part of the Community *acquis*, as general principles of Community law.

> b) The creation of the citizenship of the Union[12] brought about the recognition of a set of rights conferred on those holding the nationality of an EU member state, including the right to apply to the European Ombudsman. It should be noted that the citizenship of the Union complements, but does not replace, the national citizenship whose determination is a matter for each of the member states to rule upon.

> c) A range of rights foreseen in various places in the EC Treaty, primarily concerning the functioning of the common market.

In the face of the legal-normative dispersion of the fundamental rights that bind the Union on the one hand, and the need for judicial clarification of the principle of respect for fundamental rights,[13] including the catalogue and scope of the protected rights, on the other hand, the *Charter* has given rise to a desirable codification. This codification has brought benefits including legal previsibility, clearness, and certainty and has indubitably strengthened the safeguard of fundamental rights in the EU. The codification we are speaking of exceeds simply taking a formal shape. It calls together the most far reaching anthropological conceptions, taking into consideration what is of axiological substance: that human rights lie on a *pre-, para- and post-legal plane*, though they have a practical sense only when they refer to a concrete legal order.

132

Within this context, the *Charter* represents an *open textured* source. The interpreter should then prefer the more appropriate legal solution from among the ones abstractly foreseen by the legal norm. The criteria imposed by fundamental rights (*Grundrechtsgebotenen Kriterien*) are not to be underestimated in this legal interpretation process so that these rights can be realized in the most extensive manner, permitted by law. Hence, through the *completeness* and *weight*, at the argumentative level, which certain *ius*-subjective dimensions achieve within the *Charter*, the existence of a *lex scripta* permits a better understanding of the decision's parameters. This understanding is reached in spite of the vagueness of some concepts that nevertheless arise, imposed by the social and technical complexity of juridical life and by the need for a Community law open to social reality.

Finally, it should be pointed out that, in pioneer terms, a written catalogue arose which systematically guarantees the protection of fundamental rights *vis-à-vis* the institutions and bodies of the Union. This catalogue prevents European integration from taking a strictly economical approach and it places the human being at the core of the evolution process.

The Question of the Legal Nature of the *Charter*

The expressly assumed "solemn proclamation" of the *Charter*, inter-institutionally signed, was intended to solve one of the most discussed issues during the preparatory work of the document: its legal nature. This impasse arose out of the necessary political meaning of having a binding instrument in regard to a possible constitutional/federative development of the Union that some could foresee as "the hidden agenda"in the elaboration of the *Charter*.

In any case, it has been a pending question in so far as the heads of state and government promptly agreed in Cologne that after the solemn proclamation it would "then have to be considered whether and, if so, how the *Charter* should be integrated into the treaties,"[14] *i.e.* into the primary EU law. Following this statement, the question of the status of the *Charter* integrated the list of themes discussed by the Convention on the Future of the Union[15] so that a final decision could be reached at the following Intergovernmental Conference.

The Convention on the Future of the Union, chaired by Giscard d'Estaing, included a Working Group mandated to examine the modalities and consequences of the possible incorporation of the *Charter* into the Treaties.[16] The opinion of the Working Group was that fundamental rights should be enshrined in the future Constitutional Treaty, advocating the incorporation of the *Charter* into that treaty.[17] Accordingly, the draft Treaty establishing a Constitution for Europe is composed of two parts, and the *Charter* is incorporated in Part Two.[18]

In our view, regardless of the political solution which will be adopted at the next Intergovernmental Conference, the *Charter* stands for itself as a living legal instrument. As an analogy, the essence of a triangle is a polygon with three sides. As there is no triangle without three sides, only the polygon with three sides is triangle. From this anology one may infer that the essence of a thing is found through a number of notes that permit us to make completely clear what that thing is. To say the *Charter* is a source of law and deny its binding effect is contrary to the essence of how to form and reveal legal norms. Therefore, the answer to the problem put forward is very simple: that which is binding is that which is shown to have binding qualities. However, evidence needs premises and rules in order to draw conclusions from the premises. Thus, one will succeed in determining whether the *Charter* has a binding effect by starting from certain principles and by following certain rules. Nevertheless, this process is a difficult one: the binding effect is implemented depending on the evidence, and from the moment that occurs the binding effect is surpassed by the evidence.

One could respond that the *Charter's* binding effect exists in its own right. As well, the evidence—necessarily given through the form it is used for —is no more than an expression of the binding effect as an intrinsic part. However, difficulties occur with such a construction. The principles that the binding effect is based upon cannot be the binding effect itself, because only after the evidence is made can we be certain that the binding effect was really a binding effect. This is so because reality is *prius in animo* and, at the same time, *posterius in effectu*.

In summary, some would say that we are faced with a formal creation without substantive innovation. Irrespective of its substantially innovative content, a normative document is necessarily presupposed to have a *juridical* intention. Unless the document aims at altering or replacing another existing document, it still presents a constitutive determination, which certainly turns out to be a real creation. Further, Articles 51 to 54 of the *Charter*—the so-called horizontal provisions—only make sense from the point of view of a binding application of the *Charter*.

Henceforth, stepping up the *praetorian* protection of fundamental rights, which characterized the evolution of their guarantee in the Union, the clarification of the *Charter's* effect is still left to the Community jurisdiction. In fact, the Court of Justice, when ruling upon the cases submitted to it for consideration assumes an essential role in shaping fundamental rights in the Community legal order in the face of concrete and individual situations. It should be underlined that, pursuant to Article 46, paragraph 2 (d) of the TUE, the Court, in so far as it is competent under the terms of the Treaties establishing the European Communities and those of the TUE itself, can be called on to apply the standards of fundamental rights when it adjudicates on the conduct of community institutions.

Thus, based on Articles 220 and 292 of the EC Treaty, the Court of Justice has its own competence to interpret and apply Community rules, which it carries out according to the procedural provisions in the Treaty. In this context the Court may intervene and rule on the legal significance of the *Charter* in the following major circumstances:

1)   within the scope of preliminary issues, as the *Charter* may be called upon to illuminate the resolution of concrete litigation submitted for judgement to a national court;

2)   within the scope of reviewing the legality of acts adopted by pertinent Community institutions and, possibly, within the exercise of jurisdiction in disputes relating to compensation for damages.

Indeed, the Court of Justice, indifferent to the *Charter's* formal proclamatory status, has already mentioned it side-by-side with the constitutional traditions common to the member states and the international instruments on human rights protection.[19]

In spite of the scarce case law volume, known thus far, one can perceive a sense of juridicial effect produced by the *Charter*, which may be followed by its habitual application given its conformity with the common values of the peoples of Europe. The idea of *perceptive effect* is inherent in the concept of operative effect (effectiveness) so that, *avant la lettre* and since any court just applies law it considers operative, we may witness the formation of a sense of legal obligation as far as the *Charter* is concerned. In the last analysis, we are faced with a custom where the conviction of juridical force (*animus*) precedes the reiterated application (*corpus*) of the *Charter's* norms. Here is where we come across the concept of "*coutume sauvage*".

Considering its specific basis, it is important not to lose sight of the fact that the *Charter* implies the attainment of an irremovable protective milestone: once this level of guarantee is achieved, it will no longer be possible to retract the level of protection of fundamental rights that has been attained (*principle of non-retrogression of fundamental rights*). Regression is not possible because the provisions of the *Charter* are real legal rules (categorical imperatives and not merely descriptions of the real) and instantly become legal-community rules belonging to the same and only legal order.

The Parametric Function of the *Charter*

On account of the consensus achieved, the *Charter* integrates already the fundamental *acquis communautaire* within the lasting process of European integration.

Accordingly, it constitutes a parametric reference regarding enlargement, as the adhesion of new members cannot help but be evaluated in light of the current protection level attained.

By its substratum the *Charter* also strengthens the battery of situations susceptible to leading to a suspension of rights of member states. In fact, pursuant to Article 7, paragraphs 2 and 3 of the TEU, in the case where "the existence of a serious and persistent breach by a Member State of principles mentioned in Article 6(1)" is determined, the Council may decide to apply sanctions of a political kind to the state in breach. Such a decision presupposes the inescapable necessity to assure protection of the principles of liberty, democracy, respect for human rights and fundamental freedoms, and the rule of law—principles which are common to the member states.

Moreover, the *Charter* appears as an unavoidable material reference to the external policy of the Union itself regarding the promotion of respect for human rights in the international arena. This policy concerns the planes of bilateral and multilateral relations, including action among international organizations such as the United Nations, the OSCE, and the Council of Europe. In effect, the EU commitment to promote respect for human rights in this realm is well expressed in the founding Treaties. A commitment to human rights is a component of the EU second pillar *i.e.*, the Common Foreign and Security Policy[20], as well as on a Community policy level, both in the sphere of development cooperation,[21] and in the "new" field of economic, financial, and technical cooperation with third countries.[22]

The EU, as well as the European Communities on which it is founded, were not originally designed to promote respect for human rights in the context of external relations. Nevertheless, the EU soon asserted its identity on the international scene by encompassing advocacy for human rights and fundamental freedoms, which is a key element of the common heritage of the EU as a union of shared values. The role the EU is already playing as a defender of human rights is worth carrying out, since it can contribute to the effective implementation of human rights standards and thus to the enjoyment of human rights by all persons in all parts of the globe.

However, to play this role the EU should continue to pay attention to the call for increased coherence, consistency, and effectiveness, since it already has vigorous instruments to carry out its external human rights policy.[23] With regard to this need for a coherent approach to human rights, the *Charter* can act as a major factor in promoting coherence between the internal and external dimensions of EU policy and therefore enhance the EU human rights vision as a whole.

The Prospect for a Role of the Ombudsman

Finally, in the face of everything that has already been expressed, it is important to reflect on the role that ombudsmen as major human rights defenders may play in making the importance of the *Charter* known. In fact, while a "*dynamic reception*" of the *Charter* seems to be indispensable, the ombudsman appears as a main actor within this process of apprehension and diffusion of the content, sense, reach, and significance of the *Charter*, namely basing his positions, where applicable, upon the rights and principles contained therein.

136

As it is well known, the figure of the ombudsman expanded, after World War II, to monitor the activity of the administration. The initial aim was to address the insufficiency of the traditional controls that existed at the time. Scandinavian in origin (more precisely Swedish), the institution arose from a perception of incomplete parliamentary, administrative, and jurisdictional control, which functionally did not cover all aspects of the administration's activity.

Undeniably, the increase in and the diversification of social necessities of legislative regulation have made a definitive concept of legislation and its parliamentary monopoly unsustainable. In addition, this change has separated the administrative and jurisdictional activities, *ex ante* polarized in the figure of the monarch. With an original vocation of controlling public authorities and of monitoring the action of the administration, the ombudsman was conceived as an institution of administrative law. In general, the ombudsman is of a unipersonal nature with a non-contentious character, vested with independence and autonomy to supervise and control the acts of the public administration.

Nearly two centuries after the creation of the ombudsman, the institution followed the growing complexity of the exercise of public power. The evolution is jointly expressed by both the extension of the domains of intervention and the extension of the criteria that regulates public action. As for the latter, various criteria may be integrated into the new principle of good administration— included, for the first time, in the *Charter* as a fundamental right, owing to the *Code of Good Administrative Behaviour* elaborated by the European Ombudsman. By the same token the principle of respect for human rights ought to be highlighted.

It is for this reason that the ombudsman presently plays a crucial part in the task of defending and promoting these rights. As a matter of fact, this evolution becomes a patent one when we look at the creation of the ombudsman institution in countries that went through processes of democratic transition and consolidation. Today, the ombudsman's fundamental role in the protection and defence of human rights is recognized.

Moreover, the ombudsman's action is not limited by strict legal criteria. He may also intervene in the defence of justice—understood as the *just* solution of the cases he is proceeding to appreciate—after having examined and evaluated all the specific facts of the situation. More concretely, when acting in defence of constitutional and human rights, the ombudsman's intervention on behalf of justice is built upon the principle of human dignity. The ombudsman's intervention tries to maximize, *pari passu*, all the dimensions inherent in this principle, not reducible to a specific conception of *persona*. It is within this context that we can better understand the role that ombudsmen may play in the sedimentation of the irradiating effect of the *Charter*.

Above all, it should be emphasized that the addressees of the *Charter* are, according to Article 51, "the institutions and bodies of the Union with due regard for the principle of subsidiarity and … the Member States only when they are implementing Union law."[24] Thus, given its scope and highlighting the political importance of this first Community codification of fundamental rights as to the legitimation of the process of European integration, it goes without saying that those important functions are assigned to the European Ombudsman as well. Within the terms of Article 195, paragraph 1, of the EC Treaty, any citizen of the Union or any natural or legal person residing or having its registered office in a member state can lodge complaints with the European Ombudsman "concerning instances of maladministration in the activities of the Community institutions or bodies, with the exception of the Court of Justice and the Court of First Instance acting in their judicial role."[25] This wording appears as well in Article 41 of the *Charter*. The European Ombudsman can receive a complaint alleging a violation of the rights shaped in the *Charter*, subsequently basing his decisions on the provisions comprised therein, thus confirming "with utmost clearness, the primordial importance of such rights and their reach for the Union's citizens."[26]

Thus, the role to be played by the European Ombudsman as a human rights guardian is now of greater importance unlike the ECHR, the *Charter* does not contain its own judicial system of protection. Thus, the European Ombudsman, also referred to in the *Charter*, is unavoidably charged with materializing the common idea of fundamental rights, making the bridge between the political and legal spaces of rights enshrined in the *Charter*. In any case, in view of the political-institutional singularity of the Union, it cannot be considered that legal action before a court exhausts the mechanisms of possible safeguards for this first Community codification of fundamental rights.

Secondly, there is also no doubt about the need for the ombudsmen in EU member states to have recourse to the *Charter* in order to support their positions whenever a fundamental right contained therein is involved when member states apply Community law, in domains that fall under the ombudsman's jurisdiction. In the very same way that national courts are real Community courts when they are called to settle disputes that involve the application of Community law at the domestic level, the ombudsmen of the different EU member states can also watch over the application of Community law by national authorities in conformity with the *Charter's* norms. Also, and via Article 53 of the *Charter*, provisions in EU and international law protecting human rights shall have preponderance so that a level of highest protection of human rights it to be assured.

It is certain that the limitation of the *Charter's* scope was predetermined by the imperative of the respect for the catalogue of fundamental rights included in the constitutions of the different member states. It is no less certain that the traditions common to the member states are not unfamiliar to the *Charter*, from the very instant taking shape at the hermeneutic level, a guaranteed unity that teleologically can always be mobilized when the question of how to lay the foundations of a specific dimension integrating the sphere of protection by a given fundamental right arises.

Thirdly, even though the *Charter* is addressed to the Community institutions and bodies, as well as to the member states when they apply

Community law, the ombudsmen of other geographic regions should not remain indifferent to the *Charter*. In the light of the principle of universality, which informs the whole legal regime of human rights, these are everybody's rights, everywhere. If the *Charter* could be an inspiring element that an ombudsman, independent of his location, can defend rights that have no nationalities, the ethical function of law will be assured along with the legitimating practice of the axiological foundation-laying which is essential for any fair solution. Further, the issue is to include—within the models of the ombudsman's decisions and within a logic of complementarity between the normative and the individualizing solutions—arguments provided with universal axiological coverage in order to confer more fairness to the decision and to reinforce its reasoning.

Conclusion

The EU is evolving. The *Charter*, by expressing the common principles of European legal systems participating in a peaceful and cooperative future construction is from now on, and to all intents and purposes, a fundamental component of the European geo-cultural milestone and, considering the universality of anthropological values the *Charter* is imbued with, perhaps has relevance all over the world.

It is not worthwhile going further in indicating the characteristics that very probably will shape the application of the *Charter*. Our only intention was to open enough perspectives to gain overall foresight of what will be the profile, the reach, and irradiating effectiveness of the *Charter*— a document that decidedly places the human being at the heart of the process of European construction—or, in a broader sense, the future of this integration process itself.

Our "prophecy" within a European context is that the necessity to further find the just harmony among the values of liberty, equality, and solidarity will increase and the longing for which, we are sure, will strengthen with the fundamental contribution of ombudsmen.

Endnotes

1. *Charter of Fundamental Rights of the European Union*, [2000] O.J. C. 364/01. The text of the *Charter* is annexed.

2. As to the decision regarding the elaboration of the *Charter* and the definition of the necessary rule-drafting conditions with a view to this aim, *see* Cologne European Council (June 3-4, 1999), *Presidency Conclusions, §§ 44-45, and Annex IV to the Presidency Conclusions (European Council Decision on the Drawing Up of a Charter of Fundamental Rights of the European Union)*, as well as Tampere European Council (October 15-16,

1999), *Annex to the Presidency Conclusions (Composition, Method of Work and Practical Arrangements for the Body to Elaborate a Draft EU Charter of Fundamental Rights, as Set Out in the Cologne Conclusions)*.

3.   Moreover, it should be highlighted that those who were, at the time of the drafting of the *Charter*, applicant States—*i.e.*, States envisioning becoming members of the EU—also had the opportunity to exchange views with the "Convention".

4.   As it is well known, the consensus achieved, within a perspective of *fermentazione*, takes shape not only based on the uniformity of the foundation, but also on the institutional and procedural planes which support it, in the lesson of Niklas Luhman.

5.   On the Convention on the Future of Europe, see *Declaration on the Future of the Union*, annexed to the Final Act of the Conference of the Representatives of the Governments of the Member States, convened to adopt the Treaty of Nice, February 26, 2001; Laeken European Council (December 14-15, 2001), *Annex I to the Presidency Conclusions (Laeken Declaration on the Future of the European Union)*; and Thessaloniki European Council (June 19-20, 2003), *Presidency Conclusions*, §§ 2-7.

6.   *Supra* note 1 at art. 3.

7.   *Ibid.* at art. 37.

8.   *Ibid.* at art. 38.

9.   *Ibid.* at art. 9.

10.   *Ibid.* at arts. 48-50.

11.   Treaty on European Union, [2002] O.J. C. 325/5.

12.   Treaty Establishing the European Community, [2002] O.J.C. 325/33, at arts. 17-22.

13.   *Supra* note 11 at art. 6, para. 2.

14.   Cologne European Council, *supra* note 2.

15.   See Declaration on the Future of the Union, *supra* note 5.

16.   Working Group II on "Incorporation of the Charter/Acession to the ECHR".

17.   See The European Convention, *Final Report of Working Group II* (Doc. CONV 354/02), October 22, 2002.

18.   See The European Convention, Draft Treaty establishing a Constitution for Europe (Doc. CONV. 850/03), July 18, 2003.

19.   See *C.F.I. Disputation Foral de Ávala et al.,* T-77/01, [2002] E.C.R. II-81 at para. 35, *C.F.I. Jégo-Quéré et Cie SA,* T-177/01, [2002] E.C.R. II-2365 at paras 41, 42, and 47, both judgements regarding the principle of effective judicial protection, focusing the latter on the right to an effective remedy (Article 47 of the *Charter*). See also C.J. *British American Tobacco/Imperial Tobacco Ltd.,* C-491/01, [2002] E.C.R. I-11453 at para. 144, about the manufacture, presentation, and sale of tobacco products within the scope of the transposition of the Directive 2001/37/CE, in which is called the right to property (Article 17 of the *Charter*). In the same sense, *C.F.I. Philip Morris International,* (T-377/00 and appended T-379/00, T-260/01 and T-272/01), [2003] E.C.R II-1 at para. 122, about the right to an effective remedy (Article 47 of the *Charter*), in which the Court while affirming, *inter alia,* that, although it *"does not have legally binding force"*, the embodiment of such a right *"shows the importance of the rights it sets out in community legal order."* Lastly, *C.F.I. Mannesmannröhren-Werke AG,* (T-112/98), [2001] E.C.R. II-729 at para. 76, within the scope of which was examined an alleged infringement of the rights of defence and, more specifically, the right to abstain from incriminating oneself, having the Court set apart the relevance of the *Charter* for the proposes of review of the contested measure, within the framework of an action for annulment, not by lack of binding legal force of the *Charter*, but rather by the circumstance that the contested measure has been adopted prior to the proclamation of the latter.

20.   *Supra* note 11 at art. 11, para.1.

21.   *Supra* note 12 at art. 177, para. 2.

22.   *Supra* note 12 at art. 181a, para 1.

23.   Among these instruments stand out, for instances: the political dialogue; funding mechanisms, such as the budget lines gathered under Chapter B7-

70 – "European Initiative for Democracy and Human Rights" (EIDHR) – of the EU budget; human rights clauses included in agreements with third countries; the so-called Human Rights Regulations (Council Regulations (EC) No. 975/1999 and 976/1999, both of April 29, 1999); and the Generalised System of Preferences.

24.   Supra note 1.

25.   Supra note 12.

26.   Cologne European Council, *supra* note 2.

BIBLIOGRAPHY

Alston, Philip, ed. *The European Union and Human Rights* (Oxford: Oxford University Press, 1999).

Andersen, Robert. "Conclusions Générales" in VVAA, *Le Médiateur,* Centre D´Études Constitutionelles et Administratives, n°10 (Bruylant, Bruxelles, 1995).

Ayeni, Victor O. "The Ombudsman in the Achievement of Administrative Justice and Human Rights in the New Millennium" (2001) 5 *The International Ombudsman Yearbook* 32.

Besselink, Leonard F.M. "Entrapped by the Maximum Standard: on Fundamental Rights, Pluralism and Subsidiarity in the European Union" (1998) 35 *Common Market Law Review* 629.

Burrows, Noreen. "The European Union and the European Convention" in Dickson, Brice, ed., *Human Rights and the European Convention* (London: Sweet and Maxell, 1997) 27.

Carrillo Salcedo, Juan Antonio. "Notas sobre el significado político y jurídico de la Carta de Derechos Fundamentales de la Unión Europea" (2001) 5:9 *Revista de Derecho Comunitario Europeo* 7.

Cassese, Antonio, Clapham Andrew & Weiler, Joseph, eds. *Human Rights and the European Community: Methods of Protection* (Baden-Baden: Nomos Verlagsgesellschaft, 1991).

Clapham, Andrew. *Human Rights and the European Community: A Critical Overview* (Baden-Baden: Nomos Verlagsgesellschaft, 1991).

Colvin, Madeleine & Noorlander, Peter. "Human Rights and Accountability after the Treaty of Amsterdam" (1998) 2 *European Human Rights Law Review* 191.

Correia, Fernando Alves. *Do Ombudsman ao Provedor de Justiça* (Coimbra: Coimbra Editora, 1979).

Dix, Wolfgang. "Charte des Droits Fondamentaux et Convention: De nouvelles voies pour réformer l'UE?" (2001) 448 *Revue du Marché Commun et de l'Union Européenne* 305.

Drewry, Gavin. "Whatever Happened to the Citizens' Charter?"(2002) Spring Public Law 9.

Duarte, Maria Luísa. *A União Europeia e os Direitos Fundamentais: Métodos de Protecção*, Studia Iuridica 40 (Coimbra: Coimbra Editora, 1999) (separata).

Duarte, Maria Luísa. *Estudos de Direito da União e das Comunidades Europeias* (Coimbra: Coimbra Editora, 2000).

Fenger, Hilmar. "Fundamental rights in the European Union – Pleading for certainty in a fragile structure" (2001) XV:2 *Direito e Justiça* 49.

Gaja, Giorgio. "New instruments and Institutions for Enhancing the Protection of Human Rights in Europe?" in Alston, Philip, ed. *The European Union and Human Rights* (Oxford: Oxford University Press, 1999) 781.

Gosalbo Bono, Ricardo. "Reflexiones en torno al futuro de la protección de derechos humanos en el marco del derecho comunitario y el derecho de la Unión: Insuficiencias y soluciones" (1997) 1 *Revista de Derecho Comunitario Europeo* 29.

Hepple, Bob. "The EU Charter of Fundamental Rights" (2001) 30:2 *Industrial Law Journal* 225.

Jacqué, Jean-Paul. "La protection juridictionnelle des droits fondamentaux dans l'Union européenne: Dialogue entre le juge et le "constituant"(2002)6 *ADJA – L'Actualité Juridique Droit Administratif* 476.

Laenerts, Koen & Smijter, Eddy de. "A "Bill of Rights" for the European Union" (2001) 38:2 Common Market Law Review 273.

Malignier, Bernard. *Les Fonctions du Médiateur* (Paris: Presses Universitaires de France, 1979).

Martins, Ana M.ª Guerra. "A Carta dos Direitos Fundamentais da União europeia e os direitos sociais" (2001) XV:2 *Direito e Justiça* 189.

Menéndéz, Agustin José. *Chartering Europe: The Charter of Fundamental Rights of the European Union*, ARENA Working Papers WP 01/03, available at <http://www.arena.uio.no/publications/wp01_13.htm>.

Miranda, Jorge. "Parecer sobre a Carta de Direitos Fundamentais da União Europeia, da Faculdade de Direito da Universidade de Lisboa" in *Carta dos Direitos Fundamentais da União Europeia – A Participação da Assembleia da República* (Lisboa: Assembleia da República, 2001).

Moreira, Vital (Coord). *Carta de Direitos Fundamentais da União Europeia* (Coimbra: Coimbra Editora, 2001).

Morijn, John. *Judicial Reference to the EU Fundamental Rights Charter: First Experiences and Possible Prospects*, EMA Working Papers, available at <http://www.fd.uc.pt/~hrc/english/working_papers.htm>.

Pecheul, Armel. "La Charte des Droit Fondamentaux de l'Union européenne" (2001) 7:3 *Revue Française de Droit Administratif* 688.

Peukert, Wolfgang. "The importance of the European Convention on Human Rights for the European Union" in Mahoney, Paul *et al*, ed. *Protecting Human Rights: The European Perspective: Studies in memory of Rolv Ryssdal* (Köln: Carl Heymans Verlag KG, 2000) 1107.

Puissochet, Jean-Pierre. "La Cour européenne de droits de l'homme, la Cour de justice des Communautés européennes et la protection de droits de l'homme", in Mahoney, Paul *et al.,* ed. *Protecting Human Rights: The European Perspective: Studies in memory of Rolv Ryssdal* (Köln: Carl Heymans Verlag KG, 2000)1139.

Reif, Linda C. "The Promotion of International Human Rights Law by the Office of the Ombudsman" in Reif, Linda C., ed. *The International Ombudsman Anthology: Selected Writings from the International Ombudsman Institute* (The Hague: Kluwer International Law, 1999) 271.

Riley, Alain. "A Human Rights Charter for the European Union" (2000) September *European Current Law* xi.

Scudiero, Luigi. "Communità europea e diritti fondamentali: un rapporto ancora da definire?" (1996) 36:2 *Rivista di Diritto Europeo* 263.

Silva, Jorge Pereira da. "Os direitos sociais e a Carta dos Direitos Fundamentais da União Europeia" (2001) XV:2 *Direito e Justiça* 147.

Soares, António Goucha. *A Carta dos Direitos Fundamentais da União Europeia:*

A Protecção dos Direitos Fundamentais no Ordenamento Comunitário
(Coimbra: Coimbra Editora, 2002).

Toth, A.G. "The European Union and Human Rights: The Way Forward"(1997) 34
Common Market Law Review 491.

Toth, A.G. "The Charter of Fundamental Rights of the European Union" (2002)
XVI:1 *Direito e Justiça* 171.

Vitorino, António. *Carta dos Direitos Fundamentais da União Europeia* (Lisboa:
Principia, 2002).

Waelbroek, M. "La Cour de justice et la Convention europénne des droits de
l'homme" (1996) 32:5-6 *Cahiers de Droit Européen* 549.

Weber, Albrecht. "Die Europäische Grundrechtscharta—auf dem Weg zu einer
europäischen Verfassung" (2000)8 *Neue Juristische Wochenschrift* 537.

Weiler, Joeseph. *The Constitution of Europe* (Cambridge: Cambridge University
Press, 1999).

ANNEX
CHARTER OF FUNDAMENTAL RIGHTS OF THE EUROPEAN UNION
(2000/C 364/01)

SOLEMN PROCLAMATION

The Council and the Commission solemnly proclaim the text below as the Charter of fundamental rights of the European Union.

Done at Nice on the seventh day of December in the year two thousand.

PREAMBLE

The peoples of Europe, in creating an ever closer union among them, are resolved to share a peaceful future based on common values.

Conscious of its spiritual and moral heritage, the Union is founded on the indivisible, universal values of human dignity, freedom, equality and solidarity; it is based on the principles of democracy and the rule of law. It places the individual at the heart of its activities, by establishing the citizenship of the Union and by creating an area of freedom, security and justice.

The Union contributes to the preservation and to the development of these common values while respecting the diversity of the cultures and traditions of the peoples of Europe as well as the national identities of the Member States and the organisation of their public authorities at national, regional and local levels; it seeks to promote balanced and sustainable development and ensures free movement of persons, goods, services and capital, and the freedom of establishment.

To this end, it is necessary to strengthen the protection of fundamental rights in the light of changes in society, social progress and scientific and technological developments by making those rights more visible in a Charter.

This Charter reaffirms, with due regard for the powers and tasks of the Community and the Union and the principle of subsidiarity, the rights as they result, in particular, from the constitutional traditions and international obligations common to the Member States, the Treaty on European Union, the Community Treaties, the European Convention for the Protection of Human Rights and Fundamental Freedoms, the Social Charters adopted by the Community and by the Council of Europe and the case-law of the Court of Justice of the European Communities and of the European Court of Human Rights.

Enjoyment of these rights entails responsibilities and duties with regard to other persons, to the human community and to future generations.

The Union therefore recognises the rights, freedoms and principles set out hereafter.

CHAPTER I

DIGNITY

Article 1
Human dignity

Human dignity is inviolable. It must be respected and protected.

Article 2
Right to life

1. Everyone has the right to life.

2. No one shall be condemned to the death penalty, or executed.

Article 3
Right to the integrity of the person

1. Everyone has the right to respect for his or her physical and mental integrity.

2. In the fields of medicine and biology, the following must be respected in particular:
- the free and informed consent of the person concerned, according to the procedures laid down by law,

- the prohibition of eugenic practices, in particular those aiming at the selection of persons,
- the prohibition on making the human body and its parts as such a source of financial gain,
- the prohibition of the reproductive cloning of human beings.

Article 4
Prohibition of torture and inhuman or degrading treatment or punishment

No one shall be subjected to torture or to inhuman or degrading treatment or punishment.

Article 5
Prohibition of slavery and forced labour

1. No one shall be held in slavery or servitude.

2. No one shall be required to perform forced or compulsory labour.

3. Trafficking in human beings is prohibited.

CHAPTER II

FREEDOMS

Article 6
Right to liberty and security

Everyone has the right to liberty and security of person.

Article 7
Respect for private and family life

Everyone has the right to respect for his or her private and family life, home and communications.

Article 8
Protection of personal data

1. Everyone has the right to the protection of personal data concerning him or her.

2. Such data must be processed fairly for specified purposes and on the basis of the consent of the person concerned or some other legitimate basis laid down by law. Everyone has the right of access to data which has been collected concerning him or her, and the right to have it rectified.

3. Compliance with these rules shall be subject to control by an independent authority.

Article 9
Right to marry and right to found a family

The right to marry and the right to found a family shall be guaranteed in accordance with the national laws governing the exercise of these rights.

Article 10
Freedom of thought, conscience and religion

1. Everyone has the right to freedom of thought, conscience and religion. This right includes freedom to change religion or belief and freedom, either alone or in community with others and in public or in private, to manifest religion or belief, in worship, teaching, practice and observance.

2. The right to conscientious objection is recognised, in accordance with the national laws governing the exercise of this right.

Article 11
Freedom of expression and information

1. Everyone has the right to freedom of expression. This right shall include freedom to hold opinions and to receive and impart information and ideas without interference by public authority and regardless of frontiers.

2. The freedom and pluralism of the media shall be respected.

Article 12
Freedom of assembly and of association

1. Everyone has the right to freedom of peaceful assembly and to freedom of association at all levels, in particular in political, trade union and civic matters, which implies the right of everyone to form and to join trade unions for the protection of his or her interests.

2. Political parties at Union level contribute to expressing the political will of the citizens of the Union.

Article 13
Freedom of the arts and sciences

The arts and scientific research shall be free of constraint. Academic freedom shall be respected.

Article 14
Right to education

1. Everyone has the right to education and to have access to vocational and continuing training.

2. This right includes the possibility to receive free compulsory education.

3. The freedom to found educational establishments with due respect for democratic principles and the right of parents to ensure the education and teaching of their children in conformity with their religious, philosophical and pedagogical convictions shall be respected, in accordance with the national laws governing the exercise of such freedom and right.

Article 15
Freedom to choose an occupation and right to engage in work

1. Everyone has the right to engage in work and to pursue a freely chosen or accepted occupation.

2. Every citizen of the Union has the freedom to seek employment, to work, to exercise the right of establishment and to provide services in any Member State.

3. Nationals of third countries who are authorised to work in the territories of the Member States are entitled to working conditions equivalent to those of citizens of the Union.

Article 16
Freedom to conduct a business

The freedom to conduct a business in accordance with Community law and national laws and practices is recognised.

Article 17
Right to property

1. Everyone has the right to own, use, dispose of and bequeath his or her lawfully acquired possessions. No one may be deprived of his or her possessions, except in the public interest and in the cases and under the conditions provided for by law, subject to fair compensation being paid in good time for their loss. The use of property may be regulated by law in so far as is necessary for the general interest.

2. Intellectual property shall be protected.

Article 18
Right to asylum

The right to asylum shall be guaranteed with due respect for the rules of the Geneva Convention of 28 July 1951 and the Protocol of 31 January 1967 relating to the status of refugees and in accordance with the Treaty establishing the European Community.

Article 19
Protection in the event of removal, expulsion or extradition

1. Collective expulsions are prohibited.

2. No one may be removed, expelled or extradited to a State where there is a serious risk that he or she would be subjected to the death penalty, torture or other inhuman or degrading treatment or punishment.

CHAPTER III

EQUALITY

Article 20
Equality before the law

Everyone is equal before the law.

Article 21
Non-discrimination

1. Any discrimination based on any ground such as sex, race, colour, ethnic or social origin, genetic features, language, religion or belief, political or any other opinion, membership of a national minority, property, birth, disability, age or sexual orientation shall be prohibited.

2. Within the scope of application of the Treaty establishing the European Community and of the Treaty on European Union, and without prejudice to the special provisions of those Treaties, any discrimination on grounds of nationality shall be prohibited.

Article 22
Cultural, religious and linguistic diversity

The Union shall respect cultural, religious and linguistic diversity.

Article 23
Equality between men and women

Equality between men and women must be ensured in all areas, including employment, work and pay.

The principle of equality shall not prevent the maintenance or adoption of measures providing for specific advantages in favour of the under-represented sex.

Article 24
The rights of the child

1. Children shall have the right to such protection and care as is necessary for their well-being. They may express their views freely. Such views shall be taken into consideration on matters which concern them in accordance with their age and maturity.

2. In all actions relating to children, whether taken by public authorities or private institutions, the child's best interests must be a primary consideration.

3. Every child shall have the right to maintain on a regular basis a personal relationship and direct contact with both his or her parents, unless that is contrary to his or her interests.

Article 25
The rights of the elderly

The Union recognises and respects the rights of the elderly to lead a life of dignity and independence and to participate in social and cultural life.

Article 26
Integration of persons with disabilities

The Union recognises and respects the right of persons with disabilities to benefit from measures designed to ensure their independence, social and occupational integration and participation in the life of the community.

CHAPTER IV

SOLIDARITY

Article 27
Workers' right to information and consultation within the undertaking

Workers or their representatives must, at the appropriate levels, be guaranteed information and consultation in good time in the cases and under the conditions provided for by Community law and national laws and practices.

Article 28
Right of collective bargaining and action

Workers and employers, or their respective organisations, have, in accordance with Community law and national laws and practices, the right to negotiate and conclude collective agreements at the appropriate levels and, in cases of conflicts of interest, to take collective action to defend their interests, including strike action.

Article 29
Right of access to placement services

Everyone has the right of access to a free placement service.

Article 30
Protection in the event of unjustified dismissal

Every worker has the right to protection against unjustified dismissal, in accordance with Community law and national laws and practices.

Article 31
Fair and just working conditions

1. Every worker has the right to working conditions which respect his or her health, safety and dignity.

2. Every worker has the right to limitation of maximum working hours, to daily and weekly rest periods and to an annual period of paid leave.

Article 32
Prohibition of child labour and protection of young people at work

The employment of children is prohibited. The minimum age of admission to employment may not be lower than the minimum school-leaving age, without prejudice to such rules as may be more favourable to young people and except for limited derogations.

Young people admitted to work must have working conditions appropriate to their age and be protected against economic exploitation and any work likely to harm their safety, health or physical, mental, moral or social development or to interfere with their education.

Article 33
Family and professional life

1. The family shall enjoy legal, economic and social protection.

2. To reconcile family and professional life, everyone shall have the right to protection from dismissal for a reason connected with maternity and the right to paid maternity leave and to parental leave following the birth or adoption of a child.

Article 34
Social security and social assistance

1. The Union recognises and respects the entitlement to social security benefits and social services providing protection in cases such as maternity, illness, industrial accidents, dependency or old age, and in the case of loss of employment, in accordance with the rules laid down by Community law and national laws and practices.

2. Everyone residing and moving legally within the European Union is entitled to social security benefits and social advantages in accordance with Community law and national laws and practices.

3. In order to combat social exclusion and poverty, the Union recognises and respects the right to social and housing assistance so as to ensure a decent existence for all those who lack sufficient resources, in accordance with the rules laid down by Community law and national laws and practices.

Article 35
Health care

Everyone has the right of access to preventive health care and the right to benefit from medical treatment under the conditions established by national laws and practices. A high level of human health protection shall be ensured in the definition and implementation of all Union policies and activities.

Article 36
Access to services of general economic interest

The Union recognises and respects access to services of general economic interest as provided for in national laws and practices, in accordance with the Treaty establishing the European Community, in order to promote the social and territorial cohesion of the Union.

Article 37
Environmental protection

A high level of environmental protection and the improvement of the quality of the environment must be integrated into the policies of the Union and ensured in accordance with the principle of sustainable development.

Article 38
Consumer protection

Union policies shall ensure a high level of consumer protection.

CHAPTER V

CITIZENS' RIGHTS

Article 39
Right to vote and to stand as a candidate at elections to the European Parliament

1. Every citizen of the Union has the right to vote and to stand as a candidate at elections to the European Parliament in the Member State in which he or she resides, under the same conditions as nationals of that State.

2. Members of the European Parliament shall be elected by direct universal suffrage in a free and secret ballot.

Article 40
Right to vote and to stand as a candidate at municipal elections

Every citizen of the Union has the right to vote and to stand as a candidate at municipal elections in the Member State in which he or she resides under the same conditions as nationals of that State.

Article 41
Right to good administration

1. Every person has the right to have his or her affairs handled impartially, fairly and within a reasonable time by the institutions and bodies of the Union.

2. This right includes:
- the right of every person to be heard, before any individual measure which would affect him or her adversely is taken;
- the right of every person to have access to his or her file, while respecting the legitimate interests of confidentiality and of professional and business secrecy;
- the obligation of the administration to give reasons for its decisions.

3. Every person has the right to have the Community make good any damage caused by its institutions or by its servants in the performance of their duties, in accordance with the general principles common to the laws of the Member States.

4. Every person may write to the institutions of the Union in one of the languages of the Treaties and must have an answer in the same language.

Article 42
Right of access to documents

Any citizen of the Union, and any natural or legal person residing or having its registered office in a Member State, has a right of access to European Parliament, Council and Commission documents.

Article 43
Ombudsman

Any citizen of the Union and any natural or legal person residing or having its registered office in a Member State has the right to refer to the Ombudsman of the Union cases of maladministration in the activities of the Community institutions or bodies, with the exception of the Court of Justice and the Court of First Instance acting in their judicial role.

Article 44
Right to petition

Any citizen of the Union and any natural or legal person residing or having its registered office in a Member State has the right to petition the European Parliament.

Article 45
Feedom of movement and of residence

1. Every citizen of the Union has the right to move and reside freely within the territory of the Member States.

2. Freedom of movement and residence may be granted, in accordance with the Treaty establishing the European Community, to nationals of third countries legally resident in the territory of a Member State.

Article 46
Diplomatic and consular protection

Every citizen of the Union shall, in the territory of a third country in which the Member State of which he or she is a national is not represented, be entitled to protection by the diplomatic or consular authorities of any Member State, on the same conditions as the nationals of that Member State.

CHAPTER VI

JUSTICE

Article 47
Right to an effective remedy and to a fair trial

Everyone whose rights and freedoms guaranteed by the law of the Union are violated has the right to an effective remedy before a tribunal in compliance with the conditions laid down in this Article.

Everyone is entitled to a fair and public hearing within a reasonable time by an independent and impartial tribunal previously established by law. Everyone shall have the possibility of being advised, defended and represented.

Legal aid shall be made available to those who lack sufficient resources in so far as such aid is necessary to ensure effective access to justice.

Article 48
Presumption of innocence and right of defence

1. Everyone who has been charged shall be presumed innocent until proved guilty according to law.

2. Respect for the rights of the defence of anyone who has been charged shall be guaranteed.

Article 49
Principles of legality and proportionality of criminal offences and penalties

1. No one shall be held guilty of any criminal offence on account of any act or omission which did not constitute a criminal offence under national law or international law at the time when it was committed. Nor shall a heavier penalty be imposed than that which was applicable at the time the criminal offence was committed. If, subsequent to the commission of a criminal offence, the law provides for a lighter penalty, that penalty shall be applicable.

2. This Article shall not prejudice the trial and punishment of any person for any act or omission which, at the time when it was committed, was criminal according to the general principles recognised by the community of nations.

3. The severity of penalties must not be disproportionate to the criminal offence.

Article 50
Right not to be tried or punished twice in criminal proceedings for the same criminal offence

No one shall be liable to be tried or punished again in criminal proceedings for an offence for which he or she has already been finally acquitted or convicted within the Union in accordance with the law.

CHAPTER VII

GENERAL PROVISIONS

Article 51
Scope

1. The provisions of this Charter are addressed to the institutions and bodies of the Union with due regard for the principle of subsidiarity and to the Member States only when they are implementing Union law. They shall therefore respect the rights, observe the principles and promote the application thereof in accordance with their respective powers.

2. This Charter does not establish any new power or task for the Community or the Union, or modify powers and tasks defined by the Treaties.

Article 52
Scope of guaranteed rights

1. Any limitation on the exercise of the rights and freedoms recognised by this Charter must be provided for by law and respect the essence of those rights and freedoms. Subject to the principle of proportionality, limitations may be made only if they are necessary and genuinely meet objectives of general interest recognised by the Union or the need to protect the rights and freedoms of others.

2. Rights recognised by this Charter which are based on the Community Treaties or the Treaty on European Union shall be exercised under the conditions and within the limits defined by those Treaties.

3. In so far as this Charter contains rights which correspond to rights guaranteed by the Convention for the Protection of Human Rights and Fundamental Freedoms, the meaning and scope of those rights shall be the same as those laid down by the said Convention. This provision shall not prevent Union law providing more extensive protection.

Article 53
Level of protection

Nothing in this Charter shall be interpreted as restricting or adversely affecting human rights and fundamental freedoms as recognised, in their respective fields of application, by Union law and international law and by international agreements to which the Union, the Community or all the Member States are party, including the

European Convention for the Protection of Human Rights and Fundamental Freedoms, and by the Member States' constitutions.

Article 54
Prohibition of abuse of rights

Nothing in this Charter shall be interpreted as implying any right to engage in any activity or to perform any act aimed at the destruction of any of the rights and freedoms recognised in this Charter or at their limitation to a greater extent than is provided for herein.

CONTRIBUTORS AND TITLES TO THE OMBUDSMAN JOURNAL AND THE INTERNATIONAL OMBUDSMAN YEARBOOK 1981-2003

Professor Mohammed Abdo
"Challenges Facing the New Ethiopian Ombudsman Institution" (2002)

Dr. Stanley V. Anderson
"The Prison Work of the New Zealand Ombudsman" (1981)
"Ombud Research: A Bibliographical Essay" (1982)

Ms. Kerstin André
"The Ombudsman—Meeting Today's Changing Needs" (2003)

Mr. Bruce Aronson
"Elements of a Successful International Employment Exchange" (1986)
"Observations of the Commissioner (Ombudsman) for Local Administration in Scotland" (1986)

Fernando Alvarez de Miranda y Torres
"Human Rights and Their Function in the Institutional Strengthening of the Ombudsman" (1998)

Ms. Daisy de Asper y Valdez
"Maturation Issues for the Ombudsman" (with Gerald Caiden) (1989)
"The Self-Perceptions of the Ombudsman: A Comparative and Longitudinal Survey" (1990-1991)

Dr. Victor O. Ayeni
"The Adoption of the Ombudsman Plan in Nigeria: Background and Aftermath of Decree 31 of 1975" (1984-85)

162

"The Ombudsman's Periodic Reports—Nigeria's Version" (1989)
"State Complaints Offices in Nigeria—Coping With a Federalized Ombudsman System in the Third World" (1990-91)
"Training for Ombudsman Work in Africa—An Agenda for Recovery" (1992)
"Evaluating Ombudsman Programmes" (1993)
"An Ombudsman for Botswana?" (1994)
"Ombudsman Institutions and Democracy in Africa—A Gender Perspective" (1997)
"The Changing Nature and Contemporary Role of National Ombudsman Institutions in the Commonwealth and Elsewhere: Lessons of Experience" (2000)
"The Ombudsman in the Achievement of Administrative Justice and Human Rights in the New Millennium" (2001)

Dr. Epiphany Azinge
"Code of Conduct Tribunal in Nigeria—A Dormant Institution?" (1993)

Mr. K. Banda
"The Organization and Functioning of the Ombudsman Institution in Zambia" (1994)

Dr. Ina Barrett
"Political Clientelism, Bureaucracy, Administrative Law and the Protection of Citizens' Rights" (1990-91)

Mr. Selby Baqwa
"The Role of the Public Protector Vis-à-vis Other Institutions That Redress Grievances in South Africa" (1999)

Mr. Eugene Biganovsky
"The Experiences of the South Australian Ombudsman:
"Policy—Administration—Jurisdiction of the Ombudsman" (1993)

Mr. Ivan Bizjak
"The Role and Experience of an Ombudsman in a New Democracy" (1998)
"European Ombudsman and the Rights of People Deprived of Their Liberty" (1999)
"Special Features of the Role of the Ombudsman in Transition Conditions" (2001)

Professor A.W. Bradley
"The Case-Work of the Parliamentary Ombudsman" (1983)

Mr. Gerald Caiden (with Ms. Daisy Valdés)
"Maturation Issues for the Ombudsman" (1989)

Mr. A.J. Callahan
"Maladministration" (1988)

Right Hon. Adrienne Clarkson
"Opening Address" (2003)

Professor James G. Coke
Professor John J. Gargan
"Linking Officials and Citizens Through Statewide Information and Complaint-Handling Offices" (1981)

Mr. Luigi Cominelli
"An Ombudsman for the Europeans: Gradually Moving Towards 'Effective Dispute Resolution' Between Citizens and Public Administrations" (2002)

Professor M.J.A. Cooray
"Hong Kong's Ombudsman: The First Decade" (1999)

Ms. Katrine Del Villar
"Who Guards the Guardians? Recent Developments Concerning the Jurisdiction and Accountability of Ombudsmen in Australia" (2002)

Dr. Henri Desfeuilles
"The Control of the Administration in France" (1983) (English & French)

Mr. Ermir Dobjani
"The Establishment and Operation of the People's Advocate: The Ombudsman in Albania" (2002)

Jackson Edokpa
"Strategies for Improving Ombudsman Institutions in Africa" (1999)

Mr. Claes Eklundh
"The Ombudsman Specialized in Judicial Matters" (1998)

Sir Brian Elwood
"How to Harmonize General Ombudsman Activities with Those Related to Specialized Ombudsmen" (1998)

164

M. Robert Fabre
"The Tenth Anniversary of the Institution of the Mediator of the French Republic" (1983) (English & French)
"For the Revival of the Sense of Good Citizenship" (1984-1985) (English & French)

Mr. Charles Ferris
"Freedom of Information in Canada—The Ombudsman—The Judicial Review Model" (1984-1985)

Mr. Arne Fliflet
"The Historical Development and the Essential Features of the Ombudsman Worldwide" (1994)
"The Ombudsman's Budget, Accounts and Audit—Their Influence on the Ombudsman's Ability to Fulfil His Responsibilities" (1997)

Mr. Hans Gammeltoft-Hansen
"The Ombudsman as a Non-Traditional Tool for Citizen Participation" (1998)

Professor Dale Gibson
"Coping with Quasi-ness: Ombudsmen and Quasi-Judicial Tribunals" (1992)

Dr. Roy Gregory
"Building An Ombudsman Scheme: Statutory Provisions and Operating Practices" (1994)
"The Ombudsman Observed" (1997)
"The Ombudsman: 'An Excellent Form of Alternative Dispute Resolution'?" (2001)

Dr. Walter Haller
"The Ombudsman Idea in Switzerland" (1981)

Professor John Hatchard
"The Institution of Ombudsman in Africa With Special Reference to Zimbabwe" (1986)

Mr. S.M. Hatteea
"The Ombudsman in Mauritius—Thirty Years On" (1999)

Dr. Marc Hertogh
"The Policy Impact of the Ombudsman and Administrative Courts: A Heuristic Model" (1998)

Mr. Graham Hill
"An Exchange of Staff Between the Offices of the Local Ombudsman in Scotland and the State Ombudsman of Alaska" (1986)

Dr. Larry B. Hill
"Institutionalizing a Bureaucratic Monitoring Mechanism: The First Thirty Years of Hawaii's Ombudsman" (2000)

Prof. Edward R. Hill
"The Ombudsman as Mediator: Challenges, Limitations and Opportunities in Vanuatu" (2001)

Mr. Isaac Hochman
"Presentation to the First San Juan Ombudsmanship Congress" (1992)

Mr. Sigvard Holstad
Mr. Sven Borjeson
"The Swedish Parliamentary Ombudsmen and Their Supervision of the Military" (1987)

Human Rights Research and Education Centre University of Ottawa
Ottawa Ontario, Canada
"Ombudsman: Issues and Articles—A Bibliography" (1997)

Dr. Drew Hyman
"Citizen Complaints as Social Indicators: The Negative Feedback Model of Accountability" (1987)

Dr. Mike A. Ikhariale
"Industrial Ombudsman: The Nigerian Approach" (1986)
"The Constitutional Reform of the Ombudsman System in Nigeria" (1989)

Dr. Randall. E. Ivany
"The Theme Address, South African Seminar, Stellenbosch, South Africa" (1982)
"Book Review: *The Ombudsman Plan"* by Dr. Donald Rowat (1987)

Mr. Daniel Jacoby
"The Protecteur du Citoyen du Québec as an Agent of Change" (1993) (with Patrick Robardet)
"Comments on Relations Between Ombudsmen and the Media" (1995) (English & Spanish)
"A Social Contract on Relations Between Citizens and Governments" (1999)

Ms. Roberta Jamieson
"The Ombudsman: Learning From Other Cultures" (1993)
"Ombudsman Investigations: Serving All the People" (1997)
"The Ombudsman's Annual Report: Strengthening the Ombudsman Office in Africa" (1997)

Dr. Rajani Ranjan Jha
"The Lokayukta in Bihar: Expectations and Achievements (1973-1983)" (1984-1985)

Mr. Cedric L. Johnson
"Complaints—Grievance Procedures for Prisoners" (1988)

Mr. Ibrahim S.A. Kajembo
"Helping People Facilitate the Attainment of Fairness and Justice by Government" (1998)

Mr. Frank Kajwara
"Impact of the Ombudsman on Good Governance and Public Service Administration" (1997)

Mr. Jenö Kaltenbach
"Special Protection Requirements for Minorities: The Parliamentary Commissioner for the Rights of National and Ethnic Minorities of Hungary" (2003)

Dr. Udo Kempf
Mr. Marco Mille
"The Role and the Function of the Ombudsman: Personalized Parliamentary Control in Forty-Eight Different States" (1993)

Mr. Abraham Kiapi
"The Inspector-General of Government: Uganda's Ombudsman of All Trades" (1990-1991)

Mr. Mjemas G.J. Kimweri
"Twenty-five Years of the Permanent Commission of Enquiry (Tanzania Ombudsman Office): Dream and Reality" (1992)

Mr. H.H. Kirchheiner
"The National Ombudsman in a Democratic Perspective" (1987)

Mr. Howard Kushner
"How Do You Know You Are Doing A Good Job?: Strategic Plans, Performance Measures and Surveys" (2003)

Monsieur le juge Louis LeBel
"Démocratie et protection de la diversity culturelle" (2003)

Professor Douglas Lewis
Professor Rhoda James
"Joined-up Justice: Review of the Public Sector Ombudsman in England" (2000)

Lawyers Committee for Human Rights
New York City, N.Y., U.S.A.
Reprint of "The Price of Independence: The Office of Ombudsman and Human Rights in the Russian Federation" (1995)

Hon. J. Mr. Ulf Lundvik
"The Public's Access to Official Documents in Sweden" (1981)
"A Brief Survey of the History of the Ombudsman" (1982)
"Openness in Government Administration Versus Protection of the Privacy of the Individual, A Legislator's Dilemma in Sweden" (1983)
"The Public as Overseer of Police Activities—Some Recent Trends in Sweden" (1986)

Mr. Niall MacDermot
"The Ombudsman Institution"(1987)

Mr. Jorge Madrazo Cuellar
"New Policies on Human Rights in Mexico: The National Commission for Human Rights 1988-1993" (1994) (Spanish and English)
"The Ombudsman and His Relationship With Human Rights, Poverty and Development" (1998)

Mr. Leonard G. Magawa
"Tanzania's Commission for Human Rights and Good Governance: A Critique of the Legislation" (2002)

Dr. Jorge Luis Maiorano
"The *Defensor del Pueblo* in Argentina: A Constitutional Insitution of Control and Protection" (1995) (Spanish and English)
"The Challenges Facing the Ombudsman in Argentina and Around the World" (1999)

Dr. Barbara Male
"Assessing Ombudsman Performance" (2000)

Dr. Nelson Mandela, Q.C.
"Address" (2001)

Mr. M. Maree
"The Institution of Ombudsman in the Republic of Namibia" (1999)

Mr. André Marin
"Demonstrating Your Value" (2003)

Mr. Zvi Marom
Dr. Shimon Rozevitch
"Israeli Public Administration as Reflected in Citizens' Complaints" (1989)

Ms. Miria R.K. Matembe
"Human Rights of the Disadvantaged Under the Ombudsman" (1992)

The Hon. Mr. Thabo Mbeki
"Welcoming Address" (2001)

Mr. J.F. Mbwiliza
"The Permanent Commission of Enquiry: For Justice and Promotion of Human Rights in Tanzania" (1999)

Mr. Brian McClelland
"Oversight of Law Enforcement in Northern Ireland" (1987)

Mr. Derrick McKoy
"The Jamaican Contractor-General: An Ombudsman for Contracts" (1990-1991)

Mr. Christopher Milton
"The Wider Aspects of Ombudsmanship" (1984-1985)
"The Ombudsman as a Protector of Fundamental Personal Rights" (1988)

Dr. Tore Modeen
"The Finnish Ombudsman: The First Case of Foreign Reception of the Swedish Justitieombudsman Office" (1981)

Ms. H. Gail Morrison
"Decisions by the Ombudsman and Review by the Legislature: Rules, Principles and Policy" (1989)

Mr. Elwyn Moseley
"The New Law Governing the Conduct of Local Authority Members in Wales" (2002)

Mr. Kevin Murphy
"Accountability to the Citizen" (1998)

Mr. William G.F. Napier
"Ombudsman and Authority: A Commonwealth Restatement" (1984-1985)

Dr. Lars Nordskov Nielsen
"The Danish Ombudsman" (1983)

Mr. Vincent M. Okwechime, Jr.
"Policing the Police: The Need for a 'Code of Procedure Ombudsman' in Nigeria" (1988)

Ombudsman Ontario
"Serving With Equity: Report of a Journey" (1997)

Dr. Marten Oosting
"The National Ombudsman of the Netherlands and Human Rights" (1994)
"The Ombudsman and His Environment: A Global View" (1995)
"The Ombudsman: A Profession" (1997)
"The Annual Report of the Ombudsman" (1998)
"Rights of Persons Deprived of Their Liberty" (1999)
"Rights of Refugees and Asylum Seekers" (1999)
"Protecting the Integrity and Independence of the Ombudsman Institution: The Global Perspective" (2001)

Ms. Emily O'Reilly
"Protecting Rights and Freedoms" (2003)

Ms. Judith A. Osborne
"The Coroner in British Columbia: Ombudsman for the Dead?" (1989)

Mr. Stephen Owen
"Proposal for a Canadian Federal Ombudsman Office" (1992)

Mr. Miguel Padilla
"The Ombudsman and the Mass Media" (1995) (Spanish and English)

170

Mr. Brent Parfitt
"The Effect of Privatization on Ombudsman Jurisdiction" (2000)

Mr. Brent Parfitt
Dr. Karl Friedmann
"Little Injustices in Institutions" (1986)

Professor Dennis Pearce
"The Ombudsman: Review and Preview—The Importance of Being Different"
(1993)

Dr. Ilan Peleg
"The Soldiers' Complaints Commissioner in Israel" (1987)

Ms. Charmaine Pemberton-Carrington
"The Ombudsman and Development: Structural Adjustment and its Effect on the
Ombudsman Institution" (1995)

Dr. Viktor Pickl
"Islamic Roots of Ombudsman Systems" (1987)

Dr. Jacob Rang
"Procedures for Handling Police Complaints in Holland" (1986)
"Standards Governing Police Behaviour and the Handling of Complaints in This
Area" (1986)

Ms. Margarita Retuerto Buades
"Legitimation Procedures of Ombudsmen for Bringing People's Actions and
Class Actions" (1995) (Spanish and English)

Professor Jack E. Richardson
"The Australian Commonwealth Ombudsman State of the Institution" (1984-
1985)
"The Commonwealth Ombudsman and the Australian Taxation Office" (1986)

Mr. Patrick Robardet
"The Protecteur du Citoyen du Québec as an Agent of Change" (with Daniel
Jacoby) (1993)

Sir John Robertson
"Basis for Remuneration for Ombudsman"(1988)
"Setting Up an Ombudsman Office" (1997)
"The Ombudsman Around the World" (1998)

Dr. Walter L.J. Rosen
"Protecting the Minority: The Ombudsman of Ulster" (1986)

Mr. Michael Ross
"The Ombudsman: A New Court of Chancery" (1988)

Professor Donald C. Rowat
"Why an Ombudsman to Supervise the Courts?" (1992)
"Why a Legislative Ombudsman is Desirable" (1993)

Mr. A. Ruzindana
"Human Rights, The International Bill of Human Rights and the Ombudsman" (1992)
"The Role of the Ombudsman in Enforcing Accountability" (1999)

Ms. Catarina Sampaio Ventura
Mr. João Zenha Martins
"The Charter of Fundamental Rights of the European Union: A Landmark in the European Landscape and the Prospects for a Dynamic Role of the Ombudsman" (2003)

Dr. Ian Scott
"The Ombudsman in Fiji: Patterns of Mediation and Institutionalization" (1982)

Mr. Ross Shamenski
"Judicial Consideration of the Ombudsman in Canada, Australia and England" (1983)

Mr. Emile Francis Short
"The Development and Future of the Ombudsman Concept in Africa" (2001)

Mr. K. Soremekun
"The Media and Public Opinion As Components of a Successful Ombudsman Experience" (1994)

Ms. Vijayashri Sripati
"A Critical Look at the Evolving Role of India's National Human Rights Commission in Promoting International Human Rights Law" (2001)

Ms. Lisa Statt Foy
"A First Nations Ombudsman: Some Considerations" (2003)

The Hon. J.H. Steyn
"Alternative Dispute Resolution: The Role of the Private Sector Ombudsman"
(2001)

Ms. Alice Tai
"The Impact of Social and Political Environments and Their Influence on the
Work of the Ombudsman: Hong Kong" (2001)

Professor Richard W. Taylor
"When Germans Complain" (1981)
"The Ombudsman of Rhineland-Palatinate: A Client Oriented Office" (1983)
"Ombudsman Success in the Federal Republic of Germany: The Role of the
Specialized and General Ombudsman in a Larger Federation" (1984-1985)
(German and English)
"The Position of the Ombuds in Grievance Redress Processes of Britain,
Germany and the U.S.A." (1987)
"The Ombud of South Tirol" (1988)

Dr. Bankole Thompson
"Spatial Diffusion of the Ombudsman Institution: African Adaptations of a
European Innovation—The Consolidation Problem" (1992)

Mr. Jotham Tumwesigye
"The Role of the Inspectorate of Government in Promoting the Rule of Law in
Uganda" (1999)

Mr. Per A. Utsi
"Norway's Military Ombudsman and His Board" (1987)

Mr. Leo Valladares Lanza
"The Challenges Facing the Ombudsman in Latin America" (1998)

Ms. Barbara von Tigerstrom
"The Role of the Ombudsman in Protecting Economic, Social and Cultural
Rights" (1998)

Mr. Nii Lante Wallace-Bruce
"Ghana's Ombudsman—An Unusual Breed" (1992)

Dr. Edward Warrington
"The Ombudsman's Oracle: Critic, Counsellor, Champion—A Comparative
Study of Ombudsman Reports" (1999)

Mr. Christopher Waters
"Human Rights in an International Protectorate: Kosovo's Ombudsman" (2000)

Mr. Robin Wilson
"The 1988 Official Languages Act: A Renewed Mandate For Canada's Language Ombudsman" (1990-1991)